Praise for *BE*

"Russ Ramsey tells a stor
still haven't heard enough .... to the
facts of the matter—the water dripping from John the Baptist's
beard, the heft of Abraham's knife, the groans of a girl giving
birth on a stable floor—Ramsey brings to life the story that
brings us to life. Here is glory made visible, tangible, audible.
Which is to say, here is the Incarnation."

JONATHAN ROGERS, author of *THE WILDERKING TRILOGY*,
THE CHARLATAN'S BOY, and *THE TERRIBLE SPEED OF MERCY*

"So many authors write like they're on a mission to prove something about their own brilliance. Not Russ Ramsey. He's doing
something entirely different. Even the simple preface is a study
in a how calming, winsome, and selfless writing can be. Put this
book in your hands and feel loved."

CHARLIE PEACOCK, Co-Executive Director, Art House America
Record Producer (Switchfoot, The Civil Wars)

"Russ Ramsey has that rare gift—the ability to animate the
imagination. May you and yours take up this book, read it, and
be renewed."

SCOTT SAULS, Associate Pastor,
Redeemer Presbyterian Church, New York City

"What better way to prepare our hearts for Christmas than to
do what Russ has done so well in *BEHOLD THE LAMB OF GOD*—
rehearse the magnificent story that begins centuries before, the
magnificent story woven through all of the Bible. The story of
how God loves his children and has come to rescue them."

SALLY LLOYD-JONES, New York Times best-selling author of
THE JESUS STORYBOOK BIBLE: Every Story Whispers His Name

"When Andrew Peterson sings "Behold the Lamb of God," three worlds collide: ours, Abraham's, and Jesus'. Russ Ramsey's book opens the doors between those worlds and helps us bring them together."

MICHAEL CARD, singer, songwriter, and author of
LUKE: The Gospel of Amazement

"Ramsey deftly retells the story of Jesus with a pastor's heart and an artist's touch. In this book, real people sigh and cry, tremble and rejoice. It captured my heart. My family will treasure it for years to come."

RANDALL GOODGAME, singer, songwriter

"*BEHOLD THE LAMB OF GOD* offers readers a sterling opportunity to walk through God's story of redemption. Ideal for personal or family devotions, the stories are told with imagination, verve, and Gospel-driven joy."

DR. DAN DORIANI, pastor, professor, and author of
THE SERMON ON THE MOUNT: The Character of a Disciple

"Russ Ramsey is that rare kind of writer: both an astute theologian with a comprehensive knowledge of the Holy Scriptures and a masterful storyteller. In beautifully written prose, he takes us on a trip through the history of redemption, bringing to life the true tall tale of a Divine Lover who comes to rescue his people. As a loving pastor, Russ shepherds this great story as well or better than any writer. Not only is he that skillful, he's that full of care. Which is no small thing."

ANDI ASHWORTH, Co-Executive Director of Art House America,
author of *REAL LOVE FOR REAL LIFE: The Art and Work of Caring*

BEHOLD THE LAMB OF GOD

AN ADVENT NARRATIVE

BEHOLD THE LAMB OF GOD

An Advent Narrative

RUSS RAMSEY

RABBIT ROOM
— P R E S S —

BEHOLD THE LAMB OF GOD:
AN ADVENT NARRATIVE © 2011 by Russ Ramsey

Published by:
RABBIT ROOM PRESS
3321 Stephens Hill Lane
Nashville, Tennessee 37013
info@rabbitroom.com

Cover design by Roy Roper, wideyedesign
Cover illustrations by Evie Coates
Edited by Jessica Barnes

ISBN 9780988963283

FIRST PAPERBACK EDITION
Printed in the United States of America

*For Lisa, who tells me this story with beauty
and grace every day.*

—⚭—

Contents

—w—

Foreword

BY ANDREW PETERSON

—◊—

I MET RUSS RAMSEY several years ago in Chicago, and from the very beginning his was a voice of encouragement. At the time, he was a pastor in Kansas, attending the Moody Pastor's Conference, where I was the musical guest for the weekend. What seemed like minutes after I first shook his hand, I found myself playing hooky from the conference, walking with him through the streets of Chicago to the Art Institute, where we hoped to see a few Van Gogh paintings. Along the way, Russ told me that some friends at his church had bought he and his wife tickets to my *Behold the Lamb of God* concert at the Ryman Auditorium in Nashville one year, and that he had been moved by it. Not long after that conversation I started a website called the Rabbit Room and asked Russ to be a contributor, figuring that a pastor who loved Van Gogh would have good things to say to a community of story, song, and art lovers. That association led to a friendship and eventually to the idea for the book you hold in your hands.

Russ has reminded me often over the last few years that the work I and the other artists are doing with *Behold the Lamb of God* is Kingdom work. He reminds me that for three weeks each December, our happy band of players submits our gifting to the telling of one story, *the* story, over and over again. (And I don't mean to imply that it's some great life-or-death sacrifice on our part; in fact, it's a great privilege.) That's the same thing Russ has done over the few years he's spent writing this book: he's submitted his gift for words to the telling of Jesus' story, and I happen to know that he feels privileged too. It's not possible to draw so near to the story of redemption and come away unchanged. When a human runs headlong into an unstoppable Force, he is moved, one way or another.

Russ now lives in Nashville and is my pastor. I love to hear him preach. He has an appreciation not just for the epic scope of Scripture but also for the little things—the nuts and bolts, the lay of the land, the flesh-and-blood hearts beating in the characters of these stories. That ability to see the vastness of things together with the smallness of them allows Russ to weave a narrative that instructs and inspires, one that helps us to see more clearly what's happening behind the curtain as well as on the stage.

It's the ability to awaken the imagination that Russ, along with every good storyteller, possesses. And that leads me to the second thing I want to tell you:

I am plagued by voices.

When I'm alone, I hear them loudest. They ambush me. It happens when I'm working, writing a song with my guitar in my lap or hunkered over my computer with a chapter to write. Many times it happens when I'm driving, so I turn on the radio for distraction, but most often it happens when I'm mowing my lawn and I can't hide in the safety of a good song. I steer my mower like it's a get-away car, around old trees and across the field amidst the flapping of dark, leathery wings. "God help me," I mutter when look out the window and see that the grass is tall. "I have to mow this week."

My friend Michael Card said once that your greatest strength is also your greatest weakness. Well, I make my living by imagination. The books and songs I write are the result of, among other weaknesses, an overactive imagina-tion—one that has been abused as much as it's been used. My imagination is populated with truths and untruths, bright skies and dark mountains, horses and hags; it rings with the voice I imagine to be God's and hisses with the voice I imagine to be Satan's. The day may be sunny as spring with the smell of grass cuttings in the air, but wars are waged in my mind between the front lawn and the back.

I was driving home from the studio yesterday and the voices spoke into my ear: "Remember when you spoke to the bereaved couple about the death of their child? You prattled on about suffering and lament as if you had any idea what they were feeling. You quoted Scripture to them when what they needed was a quiet compassion. They needed peace and you gave them maxims." It was years ago, but my cheeks flushed with shame.

Then the voice spoke again, louder. "Remember how much you thought of yourself during those early concerts? You were cavalier. You swaggered." I remembered, and shuddered. I literally shook my head and said aloud, "God forgive me." But the voice persisted. "Remember seven-teen years ago, how you asked the audience of teenagers if anyone was brave enough to admit that they weren't a Christian? Remember the pride in your heart when you then told them that Hell was real, and if they died without Christ they'd burn forever? Remember how you relished the feeling of boldness, how you shrugged off tact and gentleness and wisdom and rode the warhorse of arrogance and swung the sword of zeal? Remember the violence of your carelessness?"

I remembered. And I broke into a sweat.

"Remember how you spoke the truth, but not with love? How your heart sang with self-indulgence? Do you remember when you stood on the stage and opined about the war? When you thought that songwriters were prophets? When you thought yourself a political expert? When you fashioned yourself an authority because you happened to watch the news that night? Remember when you darkened the audience's counsel with words without knowledge?"

I clenched my jaw and whispered, "Oh God! Who will save me from this body of sin?"

And the voices cackled.

I came home weary, thankful that at least the yard didn't need mowing. I told Jamie about my wounds, my shame, my struggle to survive the commute. She told me she loved me, and that God loved me too. The voices vanished. I don't know if these occasional remembrances are coming from within me or without. If they're coming from within, it may be mere forgetfulness—forgetfulness that I'm a new creation, that I have become, in Christ, the righteousness of God. If they're coming from without, it may be that the forces of evil in the spiritual realms have decided to toy with me. Either way, I'm keenly aware that I'm entrenched in spiritual warfare. The field of battle is my heart, mind, and soul, and Satan is living up to his name; the Accuser is accusing. It is one of his chief weapons against the children of God.

What defense have I but to flee? Not to flee from the enemy, but *to* the protection of the King? I flee to the one whose victory is sure, whose strength is perfect, whose promise is unbreakable, whose words are immutable and eternal. When I hide in the wings of my redeemer, the arrows of the enemy clatter to the ground, powerless. If my strength is not my own, if my righteousness is Christ's, my darkness only makes his light more lovely. Satan might as well be accusing the shadows in a Rembrandt of ruining the masterpiece. God bends even our sin to the service of his glory. This, I'm convinced, confounds the principalities of evil.

I told Jamie after that dark drive home from the studio that I realized a few things about myself. First, I remembered for the thousandth time that I need the gospel. I need to preach it to myself daily. My sin—oh the bliss of this glorious thought—my sin, not in part but the whole, is nailed to the cross and I bear it no more. Praise the Lord, oh my soul. Thanks be to God, who delivers me through Jesus Christ our Lord! This central truth of the gospel is also one of the hardest ones to remember—not just to remember, but to believe.

My other realization was that when I look back on my life as a performing songwriter, among all my regrets, all the moments of embarrassment and shame from having blabbered too much from the stage, not once have I regretted proclaiming the gospel of Christ. It is only those times when I have strayed from that one luminous subject that I've wished I had said less. No man, when he comes to die, will ever say, "I spoke too much of the grace of God." Let Satan accuse me of that. I welcome it.

I write these words with a profound sense of my weakness, but an imagination flooded now with the ringing of bells and the rustle of bright wings. The gospel gives me hope, and hope is not a language the dark voices understand.

And so, it is with renewed conviction that I here express my gratitude to God for allowing his servant to sing the story of Christmas. I'm grateful that he opened the way for my friends and I to travel the country heralding the Lord's Advent to whoever has ears to hear. I'm grateful that he has given us guitars and pianos, drums and dulcimers and fiddles and saints to play them, that he has given us voices with which to sing, grateful that he has entwined the threads of our lives and weaved that cord into the yearly celebration of so many families, churches, and communities. I'm grateful that in this book, through Russ's voice, the Lord has spoken to me again of his unbroken and unbreakable covenant with his people. May the gospel contained in these pages do the same for you.

This story is true. Hallelujah.

ANDREW PETERSON
The Warren
September 2011

—⁓—

TELLING A TRUE
TALL TALE

BACK BEFORE FATHER Abraham had any sons, the God of
the universe made him a promise. He would be the father
of a great nation, and through him all the peoples of the
earth would be blessed. One night God brought him outside his tent in the desert and said, "Look toward heaven.
Count the stars if you're able. So shall your offspring be."[1]

I grew up hearing stories like this. But something came
alive for me one night in college when I found myself in the
Middle East not too far from Abraham's desert, lying on my
back, staring up at that same starry sky. In the desert, the
night is a magnificent thing to behold. The Lord silenced
me with his glory.

I thought about this oath God made to Abraham.
Here was a man who for his entire life had been unable
to have children with his wife, though God's promise to
him was all about descendants. I thought about how hard
this would have been to accept, how improbable was the
math. And then I pictured Abraham stepping out beneath

---

[1]GEN 15:5

the brilliant canopy of stars flung across the heavens, and I imagined the Lord silencing his doubt with the same glory he was now using to silence me.

What a mercy that must have been to Abraham, for God to meet him in his doubt with this display of glory. Though Abraham couldn't begin to count the stars above, his life was in the hands of the one who made them.

Every story God tells is filled with glory. Like Abraham beneath the stars, I want to see it. I want to be captured by the wonder of impossible promises coming true. I want to read the pages of Scripture with my eyes open to the beauty of mercy and grace.

I want this for you as well.

One of my highest hopes for this book is that it will deepen your understanding of the wonder and glory of the story of the Bible. Biblical literacy is one of the most important goals of my work as a pastor. I want people to know what the Bible says.

The challenge this book presented was this: How do I tell the story of God's redemptive purpose in sending his son in a way that's faithful to the text of Scripture, knowing I must abridge or omit many wonderful and important moments? This puzzle took me through the process of embracing what this book is and what it is not.

First, let me tell you what this book is not. It is not complete. My focus is specifically to tell the story of the need for and the coming of Christ, so I've left a lot of Scripture untouched. For example, though I draw much from the teachings and language of Paul's epistles, the scope of this story ends before he comes on the scene, so I make no mention at all of this man the Lord used to write half of the New Testament.

Second, this book is not a substitute for the Bible itself. In Deuteronomy, the Lord instructs his people to tell their children about him continually—when they're tucking them in at night, when they're walking down the road, when they're sitting down to eat.[2] They were to have the stories of Scripture posted everywhere—on their door-posts, wrapped around their arms, emblazoned on their foreheads. There was the text of Scripture—the Law of Moses—and then there were the stories people told about it, those "did you read the one about" moments. This book is a collection of those moments.

Last, this book is not exclusively a Christmas book. One of the things I love about Andrew Peterson's record *Behold the Lamb of God: The True Tall Tale of the Coming of Christ* is that, while it is very much a Christmas album, it isn't *just* a Christmas album. It unfolds the Christmas story in a way which, for me, resonates as deeply in June as it does in December. I regard this as a mark of biblical fidelity. We haven't told the Christmas story well if we've limited its relevance to one month of the year. This book is designed to guide you through a contemplative season of Advent—twenty-five chapters, one for each day of December. But I hope taking twenty-five days in June to read it will be just as meaningful.

Now I WANT to tell you what this book is.

First, it is meant to be a servant of the Bible. I've packed this book with hundreds of Scripture references. Let me explain how I use them. Throughout this book I para-phrase pretty freely in order to maintain a unified voice. Rarely do I quote Scripture directly or at length. This

---

[2]DT 6:4-9

applies to character dialogue as well. If a character says something and there's a Scripture reference next to his or her statement, that doesn't necessarily mean I'm quoting the original text. I'm probably not. More than likely I'm paraphrasing and distilling a larger moment in Scripture to work within the limits of this book. That said, those references are there to lead you to the truer, taller tale Scripture unfolds with perfect sufficiency.

While I'm on this point I should note that I engage in a fair amount of speculation in this book, imagining how certain conversations happened, how particular characters felt and what various scenes looked like. I have tried to limit my speculations to reasonable inferences that wouldn't redirect the Bible's narrative arc. I've avoided inventing characters or manufacturing extra-biblical encounters. I've tried to keep my speculative input within the natural and plausible lines of human nature.

For example, Scripture tells us nothing about how Joseph felt that night in Bethlehem when Jesus was born. But as a father of four, I imagine he must have felt some of what I experienced when my children were born—helplessness, joy, worry, awe. I've attributed some of these feelings to Joseph on the basis that any young man helping his wife give birth to their first child would certainly be enveloped in a flurry of emotions like these. My hope is that this journey through the pages of Scripture will capture your imagination in ways that will serve your life-long study of the Bible.

Second, this book is an expression of thankfulness to a community of artists in Nashville who have labored for more than a decade to spend the Christmas season on the road telling, as Sally Lloyd-Jones describes it, "the story of how God loves his children and comes to rescue them."[3] With the *Behold the Lamb of God* Christmas Tour, Andrew Peterson has gathered storytellers to lend their voices to the unfolding of the Christmas narrative, each bearing witness to the truth that this story has become their own. My book is another voice joining the list of folks telling the same story, each in our own way. I thank God for the entire *Behold the Lamb of God* team and the sacrifices they've made to bring this story to the world. It is an honor to join their ranks.

Last, this book is my story. Every picture of brokenness reflected in these pages is in some measure the story of my brokenness. Every need that rises to the surface is in some way a need of my own. Every tendency toward rebellion, every cry of desperation, every prayer for forgiveness and every hope of redemption rings true in me. In these pages, I'm telling the story of how God loved and rescued me. I believe Jesus is the Lamb of God who takes away my sin.

---

[3] Sally Lloyd-Jones, THE JESUS STORYBOOK BIBLE (Zonderkidz, 2007), p.17

Gather round, ye children, come
Listen to the old, old story
Of the power of death undone
By an infant born of glory
Son of God
Son of man

BEHOLD THE LAMB
OF GOD

JOHN 1:29–34

E DID NOT have a home.

People said he survived on little more than wild honey and locusts, and by the look of him, it couldn't have been much more. He wore a coat of camel hair he cinched together with a leather belt, just like the prophet Elijah had done.[1]

Normally he was the one people stopped to behold, but at this particular moment, as he stood waist-deep in the Jordan, anyone looking at him saw that his attention was fixed on the man from Galilee headed his way. His face wore a mix of astonishment and joy as the man approached.

"Behold! The Lamb of God who takes away the sins of the world!"[2] His voice trembled as water dripped from his outstretched finger and scraggly beard into the river where he stood.

People might have dismissed this wild man as they would have any other tortured soul driven to live in the caves and wadis of the Judean wilderness—were it not for

---

[1] 2 KI 1:8   [2] JN 1:29

1

the fact that people knew his story. Or rather, they knew his parents, Zechariah and Elizabeth.

These were honorable people. Zechariah had served many years as a priest in the temple, Elizabeth faithfully at his side in spite of the fact that, well into their old age, they had been unable to conceive any children.

Being a priest, Zechariah knew the old stories of the barren women God had worked through to deliver impossible promises to an unbelieving people—to *their* people. When Zechariah and his wife were young, these tales gave them hope. God could break through her barrenness if he wanted. He had done it before. But that was a long time ago, and the stories were about people whose lives were central to Israel's identity. Zechariah and his wife hardly regarded themselves as that important.

Eventually they accepted that they would be childless, though they wondered why the God they loved and served had determined, in his infinite wisdom, that they wouldn't know the blessing of children.

Then one day the Lord sent his angel down with a message. The Author of Life was going to open Elizabeth's womb and give Zechariah a son. But this son wasn't given merely for his father's legacy. This boy would have a specific function in the unfolding story the people of Israel had been living and telling as far back as anyone could remember.

The angel told them, "He will turn many of the children of Israel to the Lord their God, and he will go before him in the spirit and power of Elijah, to turn the hearts of the fathers to the children, and the disobedient to the wisdom of the just. He will make ready for the Lord a people prepared."[3]

And they were to give him the name John.[4]

---

[3] Lk 1:16-17   [4] Lk 1:13

As a boy, John grew and became strong in the Spirit.[5] His little mind was filled with wonder as he turned over the stories his parents told him about his birth. Angels were involved, and miracles. He was *their* miracle, a gift given by God himself not only to his grateful parents, but to the world. Everyone knew John as the boy with an intensity beyond his years—as though his entire boyhood was a time of preparation and he knew it.

Not long after the boy became a man, he moved out into the wilderness of Judea. It was an inhospitable place—windy, craggy, and hot. It was also the sort of place where God had dwelled with his ancestors during the Exodus. There, without the simplest of creature comforts, John was left to find solace and companionship with God alone.

Though his days in the desert could be lonesome to the point of pain, wilderness life suited him. It was a contemplative way to live, but one that strengthened him. He had no basic needs that he could not meet. Many of his days were filled with simple tasks such as finding water, scrounging food, staying out of the heat of the sun, and gathering wood for fires at night. Living off the land meant he needed to travel light. He needed to be able to go where the resources were and move on when they were spent.

But it wasn't just minimalist living that brought John to the desert; it was his call from the Lord to proclaim the message he had been born to tell. John didn't move to the desert to withdraw from his people. He went to prepare for his role among them.

Soon he emerged as a man with a voice and a clear conscience about how to use it. Wild and fearless, looking like he had grown out of the banks on which he stood, he called

---

[5] Lk 1:80

to all who passed, "Repent, for the Kingdom of Heaven is at hand!"[6] And he did it as one who seemed to possess the authority to demand such a response.

He was, as the prophet Isaiah had said, "The voice of one crying in the wilderness: 'Prepare the way of the Lord. Make his paths straight.'"[7]

Prepare for what? A collision of worlds. Like a meteor falling to the earth, heaven was bearing down on the land of his forefathers. An old promise, so old that it had become little more than a legend, was about to be fulfilled—and nothing would ever be the same.

The Messiah was coming.

The very fact that so many people considered the Messiah's coming more of a fairy tale than a future event was, in itself, a cause for repentance. It wasn't just that God had promised to do it. It was that the reason he promised to do it was like an intimate promise between lovers. God's promised Messiah was a merciful gift of love to a people who needed both mercy and love. He would come to them in all their pain, brokenness, and struggle, and make everything new. They were desperate for this, and the proof of their desperation was perhaps most evident in the fact that they couldn't bring themselves to live as though this promise was real.

Repent! The Kingdom of Heaven is at hand!

There was something magnetic about John, something in the way he suspended those he attracted between the poles of preparation and perdition until they understood that without repentance, there they would hover—not necessarily feeling lost perhaps, but not assured that they were found either. Hope began to rise in the hearts of the

---

[6] MT 3:2   [7] ISA 40:3, MT 3:3

4

hopeless. Even in the call to repent, they heard the promise that if they confessed their sins, admitted their doubts, and acknowledged how their hearts had become cynical and jaded, God would hear them. God would hear them.

People came from all over to the Jordan[8] to step into that water with John the Baptizer. They confessed their failures, their lust, their greed, their pride. They admitted to him things they swore they would never tell a soul.[9]

But why? Who was he?

Israel's religious leaders had no answer, so they sent priests to investigate. Did this man think he was the Messiah? Or Elijah come back from his celestial chariot ride?[10]

John was clear in his answer. He was neither Elijah nor the Messiah.[11]

So the priests asked him, "Then why are you baptizing, if you are neither the Christ, nor Elijah, nor the Prophet?"

John told them, "I baptize with water because there is a man, one who stands among you, and the strap of his sandal I'm not worthy to untie. Though you do not know him, he lives among us even now, and he is the Messiah!"[12]

Should they have known him? Or, if nothing else, should they not have been surprised at John's rebuke? These were the priests of Israel, experts in the law and lore of God's chosen people. Israel was a nation with a story, a well-rehearsed narrative these priests were sworn to preserve and pass down. John himself was a part of that tale, and so were they. And yet, like so many of their countrymen, they had begun to forget the story of God's promises to them.

But it was such a beautiful story. It was the story of how their holy God had cut a covenant promise in blood to

---

[8] Mt 3:5, Jn 1:28   [10] Jn 1:19-21   [12] Jn 1:25-27
[9] Mt 3:6   [11] Jn 1:20

redeem and restore the children who had rebelled against him. It was the story of how Jacob's line came to be a nation—sometimes mighty, sometimes fragile, but always prone to wander and forget their God.

It was the story of generations of war, infighting, and exile that should have wiped them off the face of the earth. The fact that they survived all this and so much more testified to God's fidelity to his promise never to leave them or forsake them.[13] That alone proved God was not through with the story he was writing. And if that was true, it meant he wasn't through with them either.

Even though it was still unfolding, it was already quite a story to tell, and it was the priests' job to tell it. But in order to tell it, they had to know it. And to know it, they had to listen—which was why, since their earliest recorded history, every time the people of Israel gathered before the Lord for worship, the first word spoken to them was a command:

"Hear!"

---

[13] JOSH 1:5

2

HEAR

DEUTERONOMY 6:4–9

EAR, O ISRAEL! The Lord your God is one. Love Him. Love Him with all your heart and with all your soul and with all your might."[1]

Long before John the Baptizer ever set foot in the Jordan, even before the days of King David and the building of the Temple in Jerusalem, in the days of Moses not long after the Hebrew peoples' exodus from Egypt, they began their worship gatherings with this one word: Hear.

They were to worship the Lord, and they were to understand why they should. The call to worship wasn't a detached decree to render affection to an unknown deity—the God who called them was anything but detached. This command was a call to remember. They were to rehearse in their minds and hearts and homes this story—*their* story—the story of how the Maker of heaven and earth had called their people to himself and bound himself to them as *their* God.

[1] DT 6:4

7

Though it was a story still unfolding, they knew enough to understand that the Lord their God was one in number and in nature, and that the only proper way to respond to his dealings with them was to love him with everything they had and everything they were.

At that time, most of the world bowed in worship to a host of gods, believing each had the power to bless or to curse. The entire pagan world had fashioned a tapestry of religious observance, weaving the warp of the moods and demands of the gods with the woof of the tributes and rituals of man, all to win the gods' favor while keeping their fury at bay. Hopefully.

The pagan gods were not there to be known; they were there to feared. They were not there to be loved; they were there to be placated. They were many, and they were temperamental. The people lived in fear of these forces, which could lavish great prosperity upon their households but could also scorch the earth beneath them.

But Israel's God was different. He was definite, and his character was immutably fixed. And they were to love him for it with everything they had.

They were to love him with all their heart. In the seat of their deepest dreams and desires, in the place where they wrestled with their sorrows and clung to flickering hopes, they were to love him.

They were to love him with all their soul. In the place that made each individual unique, in the inner court of the mind where decisions were made, in the forming of the bonds between friends and lovers, as well as in the coming together of a community, they were to love him.

They were to love him with all their might. In the outward expressions of the passions and decisions of the heart and soul, in the places where men's thoughts turned to action and resolve turned to progress, they were to love him.

In their creativity and in their learning, in their working and in their resting, in their building up and in their tearing down, they were to love him. They were to love him as whole people, in all their weakness and in all their strength. On their best days and on their worst, in the darkest hours of their loneliest nights, and at the tables of their most abundant feasts, they were to love him.

This was the heart of Israel's religion: love. Only divine love made sense of the world. This love went beyond a mere feeling. This love was doctrine. Israel's story was a story of being kept, and the only reasonable response was to love the Keeper.

This was more than the lore of old men spinning yarns. This was *history*—an actual, unbroken chain of actions and consequences, one following the other like chapters in a book, weaving together an inseparable union of narrative and law—narrative that told the story, and law which said, "If this is the nature of your God, then love him with all your heart, mind, soul, and strength."[2]

The people of Israel were to be a people of this Law. And they were to post that Law everywhere. They were to nail it to the doorposts of their homes and on their gates, that they might remember it in all their comings and goings.[3] They were to bind it to their arms, that it might guide whatever work they set their hands to. They were to lash it to their foreheads, right between their eyes, that it might be the focus of every conversation and every face-to-face relationship they knew.[4]

They were never to depart from this harmony of story and statute. It was to be their life. They were to teach it to

---

[2] LK 10:27   [3] DT 6:9   [4] DT 6:8

their families. They were to recount the wondrous deeds of their almighty God, never stopping until the story was so ingrained in their children that those little ones not only understood that this story was, in fact, *their* story, but also that they would be able to tell it well when they had children of their own.

This is what they were to tell their children: "Hear, children of Israel! The Lord your God is one. Love him with all your heart and with all your soul and with all your might." It was a religion of relationship, but this relational response of love to a singular, omnipotent God was so gloriously uncommon in those days that it must have sounded to many like a tall tale.

And it is.

But a *true* one.

Woven throughout the story are all of humanity's wrath and greed and lust and gluttony and sloth and envy and pride—together in force with all of their consequences. But through that darkness shine the bright rays of love, joy, peace, patience, kindness, goodness, gentleness, faithfulness, and self-control.[5]

It is the story of evil against good, of darkness locked in an epic struggle to snuff out the light forever. Will the darkness prevail in the end, or will the light overcome the darkness?[6]

This, ultimately, is what the story is about. It is a tale filled with people in trouble, all living somewhere between wandering and homecoming, between devastation and restoration, between transgression and grace. Every mortal character in the story needs rescue, but they have all turned aside, and together they have become corrupt. There is no one who does good, not even one.[7]

---

[5] Gal 5:22   [6] Jn 1:5   [7] Ps 14:3

It's a textured story. But after clearing away all the levels of intrigue, conflict, and suspense facing mankind, this story is not ultimately about mortals. It is a story of divine love.

The Law of the Lord is a love story.

It's the story of the one true God calling a people his beloved, though they've lived in perpetual rebellion against him. They weren't meant to live this way. Still, they did—forgetful and fickle, stiff-necked and proud.

Nevertheless, though their lives were a ruin of their own making, God swore a covenant oath to redeem them. Everything wrong with the world he would put right. He would remove their hearts of stone and give them hearts of flesh, putting a new spirit within them.[8] And he would never, ever stop loving them.[9] God was pursuing them.

Since the beginning, this story has had an end—a glorious end. God's call on the lives of his people, ultimately, is to himself—though it would come at a greater cost than anyone could imagine. The story ends with the maker and lover of the souls of men drawing his people to himself—purchasing their redemption through the lifeblood of his own Son. God did not spare his Son but gave him for us all. And if this is true, how will he not also, through his son, graciously give us all things?[10]

The tale is a tall one, but it's true.

This is that story.

---

[8] EZK 11:19   [9] 1 CHRON 16:34   [10] ROM 8:32

3

—͞͞͞͞~—

REDEMPTION AMIDST THE WRECKAGE

GENESIS 3:8–21

O UNDERSTAND WHY God would keep such a people and love them with such a patient love, ultimately redeeming them, one must go all the way back to the beginning of the story.

In the beginning, God created the heavens and the earth, and from the heavens he lit up the earth and set it spinning into a rhythm of illuminated days and dark nights.

He separated the sky from the sea and the sea from the land. And he made the earth fertile, filling it with trees bowing and vines sagging and stalks bending under the weight of their fruit and grain. Then he filled the earth, sky, and sea with swarms of living creatures—beasts of a million kinds roaming the land, birds of a million colors filling the sky, and fish of a million shapes teeming in the depths of the oceans.[1]

It was all very good.[2]

---

[1] GEN 1:1–25   [2] GEN 1:31

13

But God wasn't finished. He had saved the best for last. In concert with his Son,[3] God the Father said, "Let us make man in our image, after our likeness. And let them have dominion over the fish of the sea and over the birds of the heavens and over the livestock and over all the earth and over every creeping thing that creeps on the earth."[4]

So he created man.

Seeing that it wasn't good for this man to be without a mate, God created a woman. And together the man and the woman were different from everything else God had made. Everything else the Maker had created according to his imagination, but mankind he made according to his *image*.

He gave the man and the woman dominion over creation and charged them with the responsibility of caring for the earth. But this wasn't what set them apart from the rest of creation. What set human beings apart from everything else was their relationship with the God they were created to know and enjoy forever.

And for a while, this is exactly what they did. In the cool of the day, the first man and the first woman walked with their God in the Garden he had designed for them. They were naked, and they were unashamed.

All was right with the world. Eden was theirs to enjoy—every part except for one tree in the middle, the tree of the knowledge of good and evil. God warned them, "Of the tree of the knowledge of good and evil you shall not eat, for in the day that you eat of that tree you shall surely die."[5] This was before death had entered the world.

But before long, the tempter came in the form of a serpent, and he questioned the woman on the matter. "Did

---

[3] HEB 1:2   [4] GEN 1:26   [5] GEN 2:17

God actually say you should not eat from any tree in the garden?"[6]

No, that wasn't what God said. They could eat from any tree they wished except one, she explained. On the day they ate of that tree, God told them, they would die.

Until this moment, mockery and deceit were unknown to the man and woman. Every word spoken to them and by them had been as honest as it was earnest. But there in the garden, the serpent spoke a sentence, subtle and slow, creating a slippery slope of uncertainty and suspicion.

"You will not surely die. God knows when you eat of it your eyes will be opened, and you will be like him, knowing good and evil."[7]

With that, he planted a question the woman had never before considered: Is God really being as good as he can be?

The woman stretched out her hand, took the fruit, and saw that it looked good to eat.[8] So she raised it to her lips, opened her mouth, and took a bite. And her husband who was there with her did the same.

The moment they broke the skin of the fruit, all of creation groaned. Lust, shame, fear, guilt, mistrust, blame-shifting, and loneliness rushed into their hearts. As if waking up from a blissful dream, they saw for the first time that they were naked. It was humiliating, so they made coverings for themselves out of fig leaves. For the first time in their lives, they questioned whether being exposed to each other—and to God—was safe. There they stood: covered, ashamed, and awakened to sin.

Was hope lost forever? The first lovers believed the first lie and awoke to the first ugly moment of shame. They were

---

[6] Gen 3:1   [7] Gen 3:4–5   [8] Gen 3:6

wrecked. Was there any hope of redemption amidst their wreckage?

When the Lord God came walking in the Garden in the cool of the day, the man and the woman did something else they had never done before. They hid.

God found them, afraid and clothed, crouching behind the bushes God had grown in the paradise he had designed for their enjoyment. They told him what they had done and how the serpent had deceived them. But it was they who ate the fruit and broke the only law God had ever given. And this broke them. They collapsed under the weight of their own decision. They needed rescue but couldn't save themselves. They couldn't undo what they had done. If all that was now broken was ever to be restored, God himself would have to be the one to do it.

But how far would he go for this? Would he deal with the tempter? How could he take away their guilt and shame? Was there anything he could do that would blot out their transgression and cleanse their consciences? Were they going to die? Now that death was in the world, would it ever leave?

All these questions hung in the air when God found his image-bearers crouching in their shame. His response to them in that moment would tell the tale.

Turning to the serpent first, the Lord cursed him, rendering him the lowest of all creatures, destined to crawl on his belly and eat dust all the days of his life. But this wasn't the worst of it. God pronounced enmity between the serpent and mankind. The two would contend against each other until the very end.

And all this *would* end. The devil's days were numbered. God told the snake that a descendant would come from the woman, and though the serpent would strike at his heel, he would crush the serpent's head.[9] It was an image rich in irony—the scheme of the deceiver to destroy the offspring of the woman would end in the devil's own defeat. The serpent would snap at this man's heel only to end up crushed beneath the weight of it.

Hear, O Israel! There in the very first moments after the fall of man, the Lord God was on the scene, acting to assure both the deceiver and the deceived that redemption would come and destroy the power of evil's hold over the image-bearers of God.[10]

Still, God told the man and woman there was no going back. From now on life would be hard. And it was. God banished the man and the woman from the Garden he had made for them and stationed an angel with a flaming sword at its entrance so that they could never return.

Though they were created to subdue the earth and fill it, now the man and woman would have to do this east of Eden someplace.[11] They would have to subdue the earth by the sweat of their brows, forever contending against its thorns and rocks and against their own physical limits. They would live off the land, but it would be a constant struggle.[12]

As for filling the earth, God said to the woman, "I will surely multiply your pain in childbearing; in pain you shall bring forth children."[13]

When the dust in Eden settled, things were different. Coming into this world would be a struggle. Living in this world would be a struggle. Leaving this world would be a struggle.

---

[9] Gen 3:15
[10] Rom 16:20
[11] Gen 1:28
[12] Gen 3:17–19
[13] Gen 3:16

Their bodies would surely die, but not right away. They would have children and begin to fill the earth. Their descendants would number like the stars in the sky, and every last one of them would struggle from the cradle to the grave as the heirs to their first parents' sin.

Would there ever be an end?

GENERATIONS LATER, CENTURIES deeper into the unfolding true tall tale of God's plan to make all things new, the people of God would enter into worship to the spoken reminder that the Lord was *their* God and they were his people.

But this wasn't due to their ability to possess God. They had no power to contain him. He possessed them—He who is One and the same, yesterday, today and forever.[14] God had not left them to perish in their sin.[15] And if he hadn't, surely it was because he meant to deliver them from it. Perhaps light would overcome the darkness when the offspring of the woman crushed evil's head.

AS PARENTS TOLD their sons and daughters this story of the Garden, eventually the children would ask about the man and the woman standing there, awkward and embarrassed in their fig leaves.

What happened to them?

The parents answered, "The Lord God made for Adam and for his wife garments of skins and clothed them."[16]

The blood of the innocent was shed to cover the shame of the guilty. It wasn't the man or the woman who shed this blood to make these coverings. This was the work of the Lord. And by the blood of the calf or the lamb, the man

---

[14] HEB 13:8   [15] JN 8:24, I PET 2:24   [16] GEN 3:21

and woman would come out of hiding and stand again before their God.

And this was only the beginning of the story.

4

NUMBER THE STARS OF HEAVEN

GENESIS 15:1–6

DAM AND EVE went on to have two sons: Cain and Abel. Cain worked the fields, and Abel tended the livestock. Once, when the two brought the fruit of their labor to the Lord, Cain became jealous of his brother's offering.[1]

Cain brooded and sulked, certain the Lord favored his brother's submission over his.[2] Like his parents before him, he tried to hide this from God. But the Lord sought him out and warned him. "Sin is crouching at your door. Its desire is for you, but you must rule over it."[3]

He didn't. It ruled over him until one day he found himself standing over the lifeless body of his brother, stained in blood, angrier and even less satisfied.[4] When Adam and Eve first rebelled against God, the Lord sent them out of the Garden, east of Eden. When Cain killed his brother Abel, God cast him even further away.[5]

---

[1] GEN 4:2–5   [3] GEN 4:7   [5] GEN 4:11–24
[2] GEN 4:4   [4] GEN 4:8–9

But still there remained God's promise that from the woman, Eve, one would come who would destroy the evil which manifested itself in every corner of creation and in every human heart. God's promise was that the line from Eve to her Savior would be a line unbroken. He would set his blessing on certain descendants who would form that line—heirs to God's promise to redeem and restore. Eve would eventually have another son named Seth. He would become the heir to this promise, the one on whom God's favor would rest.[6]

Generations later, from the line of Seth would come a man named Noah, the father of the only surviving family of the earth's great flood.[7] Noah had three sons, Shem, Ham and Japheth. Shem, the oldest, was the heir to his father's blessing, the one on whom God's favor rested.[8]

Generations later still, from the line of Shem would come a man living in Ur of the Chaldeans, "Abraham the son of Terah, the son of Nahor, the son of Serug, the son of Reu, the son of Peleg, the son of Eber, the son of Shelah, the son of Cainan, the son of Arphaxad, the son of Shem, the son of Noah, the son of Lamech, the son of Methuselah, the son of Enoch, the son of Jared, the son of Mahalaleel, the son of Cainan, the son of Enos, the son of Seth, the son of Adam, the son of God."[9]

And Abraham had a wife. Her name was Sarah, and she was unhappy.

It had been almost thirty years since she and her husband, together with their servants, had packed up and set out from Ur of the Chaldeans, the only home they had ever known. They had traveled over a thousand miles along the

---

[6] Gen 4:25–26
[7] Gen 6:8
[8] Gen 9:26–27
[9] Lk 3:34–38

rivers and across the deserts of Haran, and they had done it all because of a promise.

Thirty years earlier, the Lord had appeared to her husband and said, "Go from your country and your kindred and your father's house to the land that I will show you. And I will make of you a great nation, and I will bless you and make your name great, so that you will be a blessing. I will bless those who bless you, and him who dishonors you I will curse, and in you all the families of the earth shall be blessed."[10]

Abram, as he was called then, believed in this promise from God, and though it would mean a profound separation from everything he had ever known, he set out in faith. But it was an impossible journey. As for following the Lord, Abram had no Scriptures, no records of saints who had gone before him. Even his own father Terah was an idol worshipper. And as for the Lord's promise of land and heirs, Abram was traveling to a place he could not locate on a map to become the father of a great nation, though he had no children of his own.

Impossible.

Along the way, Abram thought about God's promise that Abram would bless the world. But he was merely a nomad who had uprooted his entire family from any semblance of security or name or place in this world. Still, the words rolled around in his head. "In you all the nations of the earth shall be blessed."[11] How?

One night as Sarah's husband sat with the weight of the world on his shoulders, the Lord came to him in a vision and said, "Fear not, Abram, I am your shield; your reward shall be very great."[12]

---

[10] GEN 12:1–3   [11] GEN 12:3   [12] GEN 15:1

"O Lord God, what will you give me? You have given me no offspring."[13] The closest thing Abram had to an heir was his servant, Eliezer of Damascus. If Abram was going to father a nation, maybe Eliezer would have to suffice as his heir. Maybe the Lord would settle for servants instead of sons. Maybe servants were all God really wanted anyway.

But no. The Lord God took this struggling man out beneath the desert sky at night, pulled back the blanket of self-doubt smothering Abram, and revealed a canopy of glimmering stars too numerous to count.

And then he told Abram to look. God bid Abram to behold the depths of heaven and to number its stars if he could. Answering Abram's fears with a spectacle of glory under that midnight sky, God assured him that his descendants would outnumber and outshine these stars, and his descendants, *his* heirs, would take possession of the land the Lord had sworn to him—this Promised Land.

Was this a promise Abram could believe? Could he keep putting his trust in something he had not yet experienced, or for that matter, in something he could never do for himself? If Abram was to trust at all, it would have to be a living, daring confidence that God would do what he said he would do.

Abram believed God, and it was credited to him as righteousness.[14] But this promise was about more than boundary lines and heirs. There was a reason for God's blessing. Abram understood that the Lord had not come to him merely to make him a wealthy landowner with many sons. This was not why God called him out of Ur. From Abram, this descendant of Shem, the son of Noah,

---

[13] Gen 15:2–3   [14] Gen 15:6, Rom 4:3

the descendant of Seth, the son of Adam and Eve, all the nations of the earth would be blessed.

God had told him, "I am your shield, your very great reward."[15] God wasn't calling Abram's future descendants primarily to land or power. He was calling them to himself. *He* was the ultimate prize.

Still, the promise did involve land. And its acquisition remained very much a question in the old man's mind. "How am I to know that I shall possess it?" Abram wanted to know.[16] God would have to work in ways that were hard to imagine and thus tempting to doubt, so Abram's question wasn't about future political or financial success. This was more about God's commitment to keep his promise than it was about the logistics of how.

So rather than simply telling Abram how, the Lord would *show* him how he could know for certain that God would do all he had said. He told Abram to prepare a sacrifice: a heifer, a goat, and a ram, each three years old, and a young dove and a young pigeon. An appointment with the Almighty had been set.

Abram cut the sacrifices in two, arranging them on the ground to form a path between the halves. This imagery was common to covenants in those days: the parties covenanting together would stand in the space between the halves as a way of saying, "May the same happen to me if I fail to keep my promise." With the sacrifice in place, Abram waited for the Lord to come.

As he waited, the buzzards came down on the carcasses, melding the holy with the profane: a sacrifice prepared for the Lord attracting hopeful carrion birds as the priest, waiting for the Lord to descend, drove them away with a stick.[17]

---

[15] Gen 15:1   [16] Gen 15:8   [17] Gen 15:11

Soon Abram fell into a deep sleep and a thick, dreadful darkness came over him. The holy terror of the Lord filled the place where Abram waited with his bloody offering. It was the kind of darkness felt beneath the skin, teeming with all manner of powers that could turn a man inside out.[18]

From the darkness came the voice of God. "Know for certain that your offspring will be sojourners in a land that is not theirs and will be servants there, and they will be afflicted for four hundred years. But I will bring judgment on the nation they serve, and afterward they shall come out with great possessions. As for yourself, you shall go to your fathers in peace; you shall be buried in a good old age. And they shall come back here in the fourth generation."[19]

Abram wanted to know how he would gain possession of the land, so in terrifying detail, God told him what was coming. Abram's people would be enslaved and mistreated for four hundred years in a foreign land. But after those four hundred years, the Lord would judge their oppressors and bring Abram's descendants back to the place Abram now stood, and they would possess that land. As for Abram, when the time came, he would die in peace and be laid to rest with his fathers.

As God spoke, the earth shook. God shook it.

With Abram beside his sacrifice in the dreadful darkness before the presence of the Lord, a covenant was being cut—a lasting promise, a binding oath formed in blood.[20]

"When the sun had gone down and it was dark, behold, a smoking fire pot and a flaming torch passed between these pieces."[21] When God passed between the pieces of Abram's sacrifice in the form of a smoking fire pot and a

---

[18] GEN 15:12
[19] GEN 15:13–16
[20] GEN 15:18
[21] GEN 15:17

flaming torch, it was to convey that if he did not keep his promise, he too should be cut in half.

Just as God passed between the pieces of Abram's sacrifice while Abram watched, so it would be for every step of God's promise. The zeal of the Lord would accomplish this.[22]

God loved his people. He wasn't ashamed to be called Abram's God.[23] And he wasn't unwilling, much less unable, to keep his word. God cut a covenant to be Abram's God and to take Abram and his yet-to-be-born descendants as his people. And he would never let him go.

Never.

---

[22] Isa 9:7   [23] Heb 11:16

5

God Will Provide
a Lamb

Genesis 22:1–14

ARAH SAT GRINDING grain into flour.

She was making the meal her husband had requested for the visitors who had appeared as if from nowhere, visitors more alien to this land than Abram himself: angels.

Abram recognized that the Lord himself was among them—an astonishing fact that would beg the question for centuries to come: "How did he know it was the Lord?" The most reasonable answer is that when the Lord wants someone to know he is with them, they know. Still, this visit would fill the minds of young and old with a sense of wonder and mystery.

In a rush to offer hospitality, Abram gave Sarah a list of preparations, and although she was nearly ninety years old, she got to work as Abram and his guests sat down to talk in the shade of an old oak tree.

Sarah listened from her tent.[1] As she ground the flour,[2] her mind replayed how they'd gotten to where they were.

---

[1] Gen 18:10   [2] Gen 18:6

This guest of theirs—the Lord himself—was the reason they were in this foreign land in the first place.

Her memories were heavy and long. She thought about when she was young and beautiful. Even at the age of sixty-five, her beauty was so compelling that her own husband worried that powerful men would kill him to have her. So he lied and pretended she was his sister. If they thought Abram was her brother, they would more likely heap honor upon him just to make an impression on her.[3]

Sarai, as she was known in those days, remembered the competing swells of pride and embarrassment that came over her during the great famine when they had gone to Egypt for food. Her dear husband asked her to pretend to be his sister so the Pharaoh wouldn't kill him.[4] Abram reasoned that it was better to be defiled and dishonored than dead. It wasn't safe, he said. She was too beautiful, he told her.

What could she say to that? She agreed even though it might mean she'd have to deal with suitors again. But if she must, then she must. Better dishonored than dead, after all.

But the irony of this charade was not lost on Sarai. She harbored deep within her a wounding secret. Yes, in the eyes of men she was vibrant and alive with beauty. But in a place no man could see, deep in the sanctuary where she would have given anything to sow the seeds of life, she was dead.

Her womb was barren, and she was desperate for children. She had been raised to understand that it was her honor and purpose to give her husband an heir, a son. But she couldn't. For thirty years she had lived the life of a

---

[3] GEN 12:10–20   [4] GEN 12:11–20

nomad's wife because her husband believed the Lord was going to give them a son, and that through him all the nations of the earth would be blessed.

But there was nothing Sarai could do about it. Nothing. The covenant God had made with her husband would require a miracle birth. For her to be able to give Abram a son, God would have to resurrect her womb from the dead. And that sort of thing simply didn't happen.

With her flour ready, she began to knead it into dough for the oven. Her mind wandered back again. She thought of Hagar. Oh, how she loathed the sight of that woman and her boy, Ishmael.

Ishmael. A surge of remorse, guilt, and anger came over her. This boy was, after all, her idea.

She knew her barrenness wasn't her burden alone. Her husband bore it too. So with all this talk of an heir and with her inability to deliver one herself, she came up with an idea. What about her maidservant Hagar? Hagar wasn't barren.

Sarai went to her husband and said, "The Lord has prevented me from bearing children. Go in to my servant; it may be that I shall obtain children by her."[5]

In what must have seemed like far too little time, Abram agreed to this, and Hagar bore him a son, Ishmael. Sarai's words had become flesh which now dwelt with her. She got what she wanted, and she hated what she got.[6]

Hagar and Ishmael may have been her idea, Sarah thought as she slid the bread into the oven, but this was certainly not God's plan. Just months prior to this angelic

---

[5] Gen 16:2   [6] Gen 16:3–6

visit, the Lord had appeared to Abram. And once again their meeting focused on this promise of an heir.

The Lord gave Abram the sign of circumcision so that he might remember God's intent: Abram would have a son with his wife—with Sarai, not Hagar or anyone else.[7] This sign was to be applied to the source of Abram's seed, and to every other man in his household, signifying that they had been cut off from the land they had come from and were now irreversibly separated and consecrated unto God in a lasting way for an eternal purpose.

Sarai was as much a part of God's covenant as Abram was. The son through which the Lord intended to bless the earth would come from Abram through her. So specific was this point that during the institution of circumcision, God changed Abram's name, which meant "Exalted Father," to Abraham, "the Father of Nations"—but that wasn't all. God also changed Sarai's name to Sarah, which meant "Princess." She would be the one to carry the line of blessing, barren and old though she was. God renamed these two not according to who they were, but according to what he would make of them.

SARAH HEARD ONE of the visitors outside ask her husband, "Where is your wife?"

"There, in the tent," Abraham replied.

Then the Lord said, "I will surely return to you about this time next year, and Sarah your wife will have a son."[8]

When she heard this, Sarah laughed.

It wasn't just that her childbearing years were behind her. It was that they had never happened, and everything she tried to do to improve her situation only complicated

---

[7] GEN 17:1–14   [8] GEN 18:9–10

her life. This shell of an old woman with this wisp of a husband were now going to succeed at what they had failed to do for over fifty years? And by this time next year? Really?

The Lord outside heard her laugh. He asked Abraham, "Why did Sarah laugh at that?"

Sarah lied, "I didn't laugh."

But the Lord said, "Yes, you did." And he knew why. Her laugh was likely not deliberate as much as it was reactionary—half laugh, half exhale. Why would God rebuke her for this? The Lord knew her situation—her barren beauty and her surrogate son.

Her laugh was the laugh of turning away. She had reached her end. Surely he understood this.

But with his rebuke, he turned her back to face him. The Lord would not permit Sarah to separate her heart from him.[9] This princess would be a queen, no matter how she felt, no matter what she thought. The One who had read her mind could also open her womb.

ONE YEAR LATER, Sarah laughed again. It was well past midnight when she crawled out of bed for the second time that night to feed her hungry, crying, rosy-cheeked baby boy. She named the boy Laughter, or Isaac, saying, "God has brought me laughter, and everyone who hears about this will laugh with me."[10]

THROUGH THE FLAP of her tent, she looked up at the stars lighting the brilliant desert sky, and she began to count.

One.

Her laughter had gone from being the laugh of turning away to being the laugh of resting in God's promises, which

---

[9] ROM 8:38–39   [10] GEN 21:6–7

the Lord reaffirmed to them after Isaac's birth when he told them, "It is through Isaac that your descendants will come."[11]

It was a new day, a season of unspeakable joy.

WHILE THEY WERE living in the land of the Philistines, Isaac grew healthy and strong.[12] Though he was still a little boy, Abraham and Sarah could see the face of a man beneath the surface of his smooth, olive skin.

They loved Isaac and clung to him like a promise from God.

So on the day Abraham came to tell Sarah about his most recent visit from the Lord, the look of vacant grief in his eyes told her that whatever they had discussed, it involved her beloved Laughter, and it was not happy news.

God wanted Abraham to do *what*?

Early the next morning, Abraham got up. It had been the most restless night of his life. The burden of God's confounding command consumed his thoughts. Who could sleep knowing what he knew?

Abraham had become a wealthy nomad. He had servants to tend his livery, so he almost never tacked his own mount. But on this morning Abraham saddled his donkey in solitude. This mission was particularly his own. Though two servants would accompany him and Isaac, no one could share the lonely, sacred mission burdening this old father's heart.

He gathered some clothes and some food and water. He cut and bundled wood for the sacrifice. And then he went to where he kept his knives. He studied them—their length, the truth of their edge. He chose one. It was heavier than he remembered.

---

[11] GEN 21:12   [12] GEN 21:34

The journey took three days. With two servants and his inquisitive boy, Abraham led the way to a hill outside what would later become Jerusalem to offer up his son. His only son. The son he loved.[13]

How could he make sense of any of this? This son was the promise, born of supernatural, divine intervention. Wasn't this the boy through whom all the nations of the earth would be blessed? The one who would fulfill the covenant God had cut with Abraham? Had God really sent this child into the world to die as a sacrifice on a hill in the middle of the Promised Land, in effect killing the promise itself?

No, there had to be another way. Perhaps, as absurd as it sounded, God would raise him from the dead.[14] Abraham held to that hope, and for three days, with the hill in the distance drawing ever closer, Abraham believed he would have to experience the sensation of plunging a knife he chose into the heart of his own son. No amount of belief in the resurrection could chase the terror of this away.

At the foot of the mountain, Isaac took a quick inventory and said, "I see the fire and the wood, but where is the lamb for a burnt offering?"

His father answered, "Son, God will provide for himself the lamb for a burnt offering."[15]

Leaving the servants to tend the beasts, the father and his only son ascended the mountain alone. On the summit, Abraham built an altar, arranging the wood upon it as Isaac watched. When the altar was complete, Abraham turned to the boy to explain what needed to happen next. With his son's compliance, Abraham bound Laughter and through tears laid him upon the altar. And then he raised his knife.

---

[13] Gen 22:2   [14] Heb 11:17–19   [15] Gen 22:7–8

He looked to heaven, then at his confused and fearful son. His muscles went tight as he realized that he was actually about to do the unthinkable. He had it in him. He would go through with this. He would.

But just as the blade was about to plunge into that beloved flesh of his own flesh, an angel of the Lord appeared, crying out, "Abraham! Abraham! Do not lay a hand on the boy."[16]

Abraham looked up and couldn't believe what he saw. How had he not noticed it before? Incarnate before him, caught by its horns in a nearby thicket, stood a ram, as if it were sent to ascend this hill from the other side for the purpose of dying in order that Laughter might live.

"Abraham took the ram and offered it up as a burnt offering instead of his son."[17] And the angel appeared again, with a message: "By myself I have sworn, declares the Lord, that because you have done this and have not withheld your son, your only son, I will surely bless you, and I will surely multiply your offspring as the stars of heaven and as the sand that is on the seashore. And your offspring shall possess the gate of his enemies, and in your offspring shall all the nations of the earth be blessed, because you have obeyed my voice."[18]

This message wasn't new, and that as much as anything made it ring like a sweet song in Abraham's ears. It was the same covenant oath the Lord had sworn since the very beginning, and God had shown himself faithful.

---

[16] Gen 22:11–12   [17] Gen 22:13   [18] Gen 22:16–18

6

JACOB AND TWO WOMEN

GENESIS 27:1–29

HE ENTIRE TIME he lived in the land promised to his descendants, Abraham never owned so much as an acre. Nor would he until he bought the field near Machpelah for his beloved Sarah.

If the defining moments in Abraham's life were captured as stills on canvas, each picture would be of a place miles away from the one before and from the one to follow. They would depict a journey with ever-changing geography, faces, and definition. Yet there was one constant for Abraham in every memory and moment: Sarah, lovely and dignified, filled with passion and imagination. She bore her husband's burdens as though they were her own. This journey was her story too, and Abraham loved her for it.

But now the mother of his son, Isaac, this woman the Lord had renamed "Princess" and then made into a queen, had died.

So Abraham went to some of the wealthy rulers in the land, the Hittites, to buy a place to bury his wife.[1] Knowing

---
[1] GEN 23:3–4

Abraham had become very wealthy in his own right, the Hittites said, "Hear us, my lord; you are a prince of God among us. Bury your dead in the choicest of our tombs. None of us will withhold from you his tomb to hinder you from burying your dead."[2]

Of course no tomb would really be free. It would be a loan that would become leverage for future favors. Abraham didn't want to borrow. He wanted to own. He didn't want to become beholden to the Hittites over the ownership of his beloved's grave. So when Ephron, the owner of the cave Abraham wanted, offered to loan it to him indefinitely, Abraham declined.

Instead, he asked Ephron to name the price he wanted. If Ephron got his initial asking price without having to haggle, this would publicly verify that Abraham acquired the cave honestly and fairly. Ephron wanted four hundred shekels of silver, and Abraham paid it.[3] The tomb, the field the tomb was in, and the fence around it were all deeded to Abraham.

And so it was, at last, that the Father of Nations took his first possession of the land the Lord swore to his descendants.[4] It wasn't a fertile valley or a palace or a vineyard. It was a burial site. And there he buried the wife of his youth, his queen, his beloved Sarah.

ISAAC LIVED WITH his father until his mid-thirties.[5] As Abraham watched his son grow older, he wanted him to find a wife, one who would remind Isaac of his mother—a woman from Sarah's own homeland, someone willing to follow her husband wherever the Lord might lead them.[6]

---

[2] GEN 23:6   [4] GEN 23:17–20   [6] GEN 24:1–9
[3] GEN 23:14   [5] GEN 25:20

Abraham sent one of his servants back to Mesopotamia to find a woman from Sarah's clan for Isaac. Through a providential encounter, Abraham's servant met a young woman named Rebekah and told her why he had come. One of Rebekah's maidservants ran home to tell Rebekah's brother Laban about this man who hoped to find a wife for his master's son.

Laban ran to meet the man and to see if he represented a wealthy family. The bracelets the servant offered and the camels kneeling at Laban's well looked promising.[7] Abraham's servant wanted Rebekah to return with him. Laban did as well. So Rebekah agreed to go.[8]

Isaac loved Rebekah. Like his mother, Rebekah was from the area of Paddan-Aram. Like Sarah, she was willing to go wherever the Lord led. And like his mother at her age, Rebekah was beautiful—and barren.

Isaac prayed that the Lord would do for his wife what he had done for his mother. He prayed God would open her womb and give them a son.[9]

The Lord answered his prayer, and Rebekah conceived not one boy, but two. The Lord told her, "Two nations are in your womb, and the two peoples from within you shall be divided. One shall be stronger than the other, and the older shall serve the younger."[10] Whenever she prayed for them, the boys struggled in her belly as though their wrestling had already begun.

Esau came into the world first, red and covered in hair. His brother followed, clutching Esau's heel, as though even from within the womb he was playing the angles, trying to figure out a way to pull ahead. They named this one Jacob,

---

[7] GEN 24:30

[8] GEN 24:50–59

[9] GEN 25:21

[10] GEN 25:23

which meant "one who grabs at the heel," another word for "deceiver" or "cheater."[11]

Esau grew into a rugged outdoorsman, and his father favored him because Esau kept Isaac's plate filled with fresh game. Jacob, on the other hand, tended to stay around the camp, and Rebekah loved him for it.[12]

As Isaac's eyesight faded with age, he wanted to pass along to Esau, his firstborn, the family blessing—the blessing of Seth and Noah. The blessing God had set upon Abraham, which had been passed on to Isaac.[13]

Though Isaac intended to give Esau his blessing, Rebekah wanted it to go to Jacob. She conspired with Jacob to trick the old man into giving it to him instead. She would prepare Isaac's favorite meal and then have Jacob bring it to him wearing furs on his arms and his brother's clothes on his back so he would feel and smell like Esau.[14]

Their plan worked. While Esau was out hunting, Jacob brought Isaac the meal his mother had prepared. Though it took a bit of convincing, Jacob did eventually persuade his father that the man standing in front of him who felt and smelled like Esau must be Esau.

Isaac named Jacob his heir, giving him the full family blessing—the covenant promise the Lord had bestowed on his father, the promise to become a great people through which all the nations of the earth would be blessed.[15]

When Esau discovered that he had been swindled out of his birthright, rage overcame him and he swore to exact revenge on his heel-grabbing little brother. Given the chance, he would kill Jacob. Rebekah heard Esau's eruption and told Jacob he had better make himself scarce.

---

[11] GEN 25:26   [13] GEN 26:2–5   [15] GEN 27:28–29
[12] GEN 25:27   [14] GEN 27:1–29

Maybe he should seek asylum with her brother Laban, at least until Esau cooled off.[16] And maybe while he was there, he could do what his own father had done. Maybe he could find himself a wife.[17]

What Jacob didn't know was that his uncle Laban was every bit the cheater he was. Knowing Jacob descended from great wealth, Laban did everything he could to relieve Jacob of as much of that wealth as possible while giving Jacob as much of his own burden as Jacob would willingly bear.

Jacob fell in love with one of Laban's daughters— Rachel. He wanted to marry her, so he offered to work as Laban's servant for seven years in exchange for Laban's daughter's hand in marriage.

Laban was happy to oblige. But when the day of the wedding came, the woman under the bridal veil taking Jacob as her husband was not Rachel, but Laban's other daughter, Leah.

"Oh," Laban feigned. "You meant Rachel? You know, in our culture, we don't permit the younger daughter to marry first. Didn't you know that? I'll tell you what: for another seven years of servitude, you can marry Rachel too."[18]

Though Jacob had clearly been tricked into taking both of Laban's daughters off his hands, his love for Rachel was strong. He would do whatever it took to bring her home as his wife. So Jacob worked for Laban another seven years.[19]

But Laban wasn't the only schemer. Jacob quietly worked to build his herds and possessions until his personal wealth rivaled that of his uncle. Jacob even managed to trick Laban out of most of his own livestock.[20]

---

[16] GEN 27:42–45
[17] GEN 28:1–5
[18] GEN 29:26–27
[19] GEN 29:28–30
[20] GEN 30:25–43

Though their relationship was an ongoing struggle, neither Jacob nor Laban could really argue with the results. Both knew they lived to swindle the other, and within that system existed a sort of code which said that if one schemer was foolish enough to fall for another's scheme, then that was his fault.

Still, they had to find a way to live at peace. Eventually Jacob concluded that living at peace with his uncle Laban meant living apart from him. So Jacob gathered his wives, his servants, his children, his livestock, and all their possessions and set out for the only other home he knew—the land of his father in Canaan.[21]

Only it wasn't the land of his father anymore. It was the land of his brother, and the last Jacob had heard, Esau had sworn to kill him.[22]

---

[21] GEN 31:17–18   [22] GEN 27:42

7

WALKING WITH
A LIMP

GENESIS 32:22–32

ACOB HOPED HIS path would never cross Esau's again. But it would, and soon. Though it had been years, Jacob had no reason to think Esau had forgotten his trickery.

As he drew near the land of his youth, he sent a party of scouts ahead to intercept Esau, lavish him with gifts, and let him know Jacob was coming. And hopefully somewhere in all of this, they might be able to gauge Esau's reaction.

Soon the scouts returned and told Jacob they had found Esau. He was coming out to meet them. And he was bringing a small army.[1]

Dread swept over Jacob. He turned to the Lord. "I'm not worthy of the least of all the deeds of steadfast love and all the faithfulness that you have shown to your servant... Please deliver me from the hand of my brother, from the hand of Esau, for I fear him. I'm afraid that he might come and attack me."[2]

---

[1] GEN 32:6   [2] GEN 32:10–11

But even as he prayed, Jacob was doing what he did best—scheming. He crossed the Jabbok River and separated his caravan into two camps so that if Esau attacked one, the other could either help or run. He sent his wives and children to the other side of the river so that, regardless of which camp Esau attacked, Leah, Rachel, and the kids would be safely hidden in the canyons of the Jabbok.[3] Then he assembled three more parties of scouts, each with herds of livestock to offer as gifts, and dispatched them one after another like waves of blessing and prosperity that might break over his brother and smooth any roughness between them.

WITH EVERYONE IN place, Jacob waited by the banks of the Jabbok, alone in the dark. He was no stranger to trouble. He had been tricking people and reaping the whirlwind for as long as he could remember. He and this river were not that different. All through his life, his schemes, like streams of water, gathered from high and hidden places and flowed together to cut their way through whatever lines of weakness they could find. Jacob never saw much beyond the headwaters of his own schemes, but their consequences spread like tributaries, cutting channels through his victims' weaknesses. He had lived his entire life this way. Sooner or later, there would be a reckoning.

And now Esau was coming.

THERE IN THE dark, Jacob sat alone, wondering what Esau was hungry for. Whatever it was, Jacob knew his brother would follow his appetites. Esau's anger centered on Jacob stealing his birthright. But even before that, when they

---

[3] GEN 32:6–20

were younger, Esau had offered it to Jacob in exchange for a bowl of stew.[4]

It was such a foolish thing to do. All their lives, their father and grandfather had told them that in their family, the birthright was everything. God was working through this family to bless the earth. He was establishing the lineage through which the great Redeemer would come. To carry the birthright of this family was to stand in an unbreakable line that would one day give this world a Savior.

To brazenly trade it away just to fill his belly was unbelievably foolish. Though Jacob's deceit was unfair to Isaac, Esau had forfeited that birthright to Jacob years before. Though no one could fault Esau for being angry, this was a mess of his own making.

But that offered little comfort now. Jacob wondered if the dawn would bring on the fight of his life.

THEN, FROM NOWHERE, a strong hand grabbed Jacob and threw him to the ground. Where his assailant had come from or who he was, Jacob didn't know. Whoever he was, he was strong, and he was winning.

Adrenaline shot through Jacob's veins, and he did the only thing he could. He fought back. Jacob wrestled with every bit of strength he had, with every muscle and with every wit. It was exhausting, but alone in the dark, what were his options? Surrender? Surely Jacob, the son of Isaac, the Son of Abraham, the friend of God,[5] had the Lord on his side. Surely the Almighty would give Jacob the strength to prevail.

Whatever petitions he might have whispered for the Lord's help were uttered in beautiful irony. He didn't know

---

[4] GEN 25:29–34   [5] JAS 2:23

that the God to whom he prayed was the very one who now had him tangled up in the dirt.

But Jacob stayed in the fight. As the first signs of morning glowed in the east, the Lord knocked Jacob's hip—the core of a wrestler's strength, the pivot point—out of its socket. Whatever leverage Jacob might have had was gone. After that, it must have seemed like Jacob's opponent was toying with him, wearing him down.

But the Lord was not out to destroy Jacob. He was out to break him. Jacob had gone from wrestling to clinging, and he held onto the Lord as though his life depended on it.

The Lord said, "Let me go."

Jacob said, "I won't let you go unless you bless me."[6] Jacob didn't want to leave this fight wondering when the next would be. He knew he couldn't win. He knew he was at the mercy of the Lord. So Jacob cried out for the blessing he had tried to steal from his brother and take from his father. He wanted that blessing.

So the Lord asked him, "What is your name?"[7] God has never asked a question because he lacked information. He wanted Jacob to take the stand and testify against himself before the court of the Most High. He wanted Jacob to confess that he was the son of Isaac, the grandson of Abraham, and the heir of God's covenant promises. And he wanted Jacob to confess that he was a deceiver and a cheat.

"Who are you, Jacob?"

With his strength spent, his hip dislocated, and his last wit frayed, the broken man declared, "I am Jacob, the heel-grabber."[8]

God promised Adam and Eve that life would be a struggle. Jacob's whole life had been marked by struggles

---

[6] GEN 32:26   [7] GEN 32:27   [8] GEN 32:27

of his own making. He came out of the womb scheming, and he never looked back. He wrestled the birthright from his brother, the blessing from his father, and two brides from his uncle.

He knew he was a good schemer. He could wrestle away pretty much anything he wanted from anyone he chose. All he ever did was wrestle. Still, none of it made him happy, and none of it brought him peace.

But now, exhausted and stripped of leverage, he had nothing left but to cling to God for his blessing. A flicker of hope sparked in Jacob as he realized there would be no stealing it this time. He couldn't wrestle anything away from God. Even with all his wealth and family and ambition, in this moment nothing mattered except who he was before God.

He was all at once fragile. Maybe he could finally know peace. Maybe now he could yield. Though his brother could trade it and his father could speak it, only God could bless him. Only God could actually do what he had promised.

The angel of the Lord spoke a blessing over Jacob, saying, "From now on, your name shall no longer be Jacob (Deceiver) but Israel (God fights) because you have striven with God and with men and have prevailed."[9]

As Jacob, he was the scheming son of Isaac. But as Israel, he would become the namesake of the nation the Lord swore to make of his grandfather Abraham's seed. The nation through which all other nations of the earth would be blessed would take his name, the name God had given him. They would be Israel.

And as history would show, they would be just like their namesake—stiff-necked and proud, prone to schemes and

[9] GEN 32:28

47

eager to bargain. Though they would wrestle with God, and though the Lord would hobble them, stripping them of their leverage, it would be because God was fighting for them even when they were fighting against him, even when they forgot the covenant the Lord himself swore to uphold.

Their forefather Israel walked before God with a limp. And they would too. But the Lord would uphold them. They would belong to him.

8

Four Hundred Years

Genesis 50:15–21

HE SWEAT ON Esau's brow dripped down the side of his face as he squinted through the heat. The sun on the sand made the desert shimmer like the sea. The four hundred men with him knew their mission might turn violent, but they couldn't read Esau's intentions any better than he could read them himself. He didn't know what to feel. He walked ahead, alone with his thoughts—a small army behind him and a full-blown war raging in his heart.

Before long a figure emerged from the mirage, limping toward him. When the man came closer, he dropped to his knees. Behind him stood an army of his own, made up mostly of women and children.

Esau knew this man. He knew him well. It was his brother Jacob—his twin. Esau had plenty of reasons to want his brother dead. Many times he had rehearsed what he would say given the opportunity. But in this moment, the only words that would come to his lips were, "Who are all these people with you?"[1]

---

[1] Gen 33:5

49

He knew who they were. They were his sisters-in-law, his nieces, his nephews, *his* family. Esau wept. These were the loved ones God had graciously given his brother. And in this reunion in the desert, perhaps Esau couldn't help but feel that God was giving them to him too.

The healing that took place brought two warring brothers to a rare moment of peace. With the blessing of his brother, Jacob went from that meeting to settle his family in the region near Bethlehem. He was back in the land of his fathers. Israel was going home.

Rachel was in the late stages of pregnancy while their caravan traveled to Bethlehem. Along the way, as her delivery drew near, Rachel, the midwives, and Jacob all knew something was wrong. The color was draining from Rachel's face. Travel was difficult for her, so they stopped. As labor set in, beads of sweat glistened on her forehead. Even as her baby boy was being born, she was fading.

The midwife told her the child was a boy, and Rachel whispered with her dying breath, "Call him Ben-oni, the son of my sorrow."

But Israel wouldn't have it. He said, "This child will not carry a name to remind me of my grief. He will be called Benjamin, the son of my right hand."

JACOB AND LEAH and the rest of their family settled in the land near Bethlehem. They kept a busy home full of boys growing into men. The brothers fought with each other like little lions, but they also would have given up their lives for each other. Except for one.

Benjamin had eleven older brothers, and they all knew Jacob favored one of them over the rest. His name was Joseph. Jacob doted on Joseph and set him apart by giving him a brightly colored robe, which Joseph wore with pride.

It wasn't so much the robe as it was their father's unapologetic favoritism that really ate at Joseph's brothers. They hated Joseph for this so much that they conspired together to get rid of him for good. They sold him as a slave to a caravan of Ishmaelites for twenty shekels of silver,[2] and the caravan trundled away over the desert slopes, taking the frightened boy from the land of his father to Egypt.

The brothers returned home to tell their father that Joseph had died. Jacob's heart broke. The boy he loved so much had vanished from his life, and there was nothing Jacob could do to get him back.

Joseph's heart broke too. He had gone from being a beloved son to being a piece of property purchased by a man named Potiphar, who made him a servant in his home.

Potiphar's wife developed an attraction to Joseph and tried many times to seduce him. Joseph resisted her with words until her advances became physical. One day when she and Joseph were alone in the house, she grabbed him and tried to pull him into her arms. Joseph fled, leaving the scorned wife holding his robe in her hand. Angry and humiliated, Potiphar's wife yelled for help, accusing Joseph of trying to take advantage of her. Joseph, being a foreigner and a slave, had no hope of defending himself, and he was thrown into prison.[3]

In prison, Joseph came to be known as a man blessed with God's vision. When people were troubled by strange dreams, Joseph could explain them. The king of Egypt began having nightmares about skinny cows eating up the fattened ones. He needed to understand what the dreams

---

[2] GEN 37   [3] GEN 39:1–23

meant, so he asked his sorcerers and magicians. No one could help him.[4]

The pharaoh's royal cupbearer remembered how Joseph had interpreted a dream for him and told the king about him. The pharaoh summoned Joseph for an interpretation, and Joseph told him this dream was God's way of warning them of a coming famine and that he could help the pharaoh prepare for it. So Joseph went from being an imprisoned slave to being a ruler in the land, second only to the king himself, saving the kingdom through an aggressive food-storage program.[5]

The famine was severe, and the entire region suffered under it, but unlike Egypt, few had prepared for it. Neighboring countries' food supplies dried up, leaving them in a desperate crisis. People heard about Joseph's storehouses and came hungry, hoping for some of Egypt's reserve. The pharaoh put Joseph over the distribution, leaving him in charge of what was left of the world's food supply.[6]

Joseph's brothers languished in nearby Canaan with their aging father Israel. Soon they too came looking for food. Enough time had passed since they sold their brother into slavery that the boy had become a man, and by all appearances an Egyptian man. To his brothers, Joseph looked like a prince, rich and powerful. And all they knew about him was that this prince held the key to their survival.

With his brothers standing before him, gaunt and desperate, Joseph had a choice. Not only had they sold him out of their family, they didn't even recognize his face. Was he so dead to them that even their memory of him was gone? His eyes burned with tears, but he decided to keep his identity from them. He questioned them about their

---

[4] GEN 41:24   [5] GEN 39–41   [6] GEN 41:55

family. They had another brother, and their father was old and frail. Without the prince's help, they would not survive.

Joseph tested them at length. He wanted to know how the years had shaped their character. He didn't know exactly what he was testing them for, but what he found was that he still loved them. His brothers needed his help, and he wanted to give it. The prince cleared his throat and spoke to them with a familiar voice that opened their eyes and broke their hearts: "Brothers, it's me! I'm Joseph."[7]

His brothers stood there, stunned, not sure what was happening. The one they had tried to kill was saving their lives. The only hope they could latch onto in that moment was that Joseph's love for them was greater than their guilt over the evil they had done.

"I will provide for you. You will not be lost. I will bring you under the protection and provision of the house of Pharaoh himself." Joseph embraced his brothers, and together they wept for joy.

When the pharaoh heard that Joseph's brothers had come, it pleased him. To honor the man who had saved their nation from ruin, the pharaoh told Joseph to bring his entire family into the region of Goshen, where they could live off the fat of the land, never again lacking anything.[8] So Joseph moved his family to Egypt where they would live off the provisions the Lord had used him to store up.[9]

What Joseph's brothers meant for evil, God meant for good.[10] God meant for this prince, whose heart had been broken by his own people, to save them. And God meant to bring these people—the ones he had called to himself as his own—out of their peril and hunger and into a place

---

[7] GEN 45:3
[8] GEN 45:16–20
[9] GEN 42–50
[10] GEN 50:20

where they would have to connect in their minds the life-giving provision of the king with the unearned mercy and grace of the prince. Though the brothers meant to kill the prince, he gave them life in his name—life to the fullest.[11]

THE YEARS PASSED, and Jacob's sons flourished in the land of Goshen, but Egypt was not their home. When Joseph grew old, he told his brothers, "I'm about to die, but God will visit you and bring you up out of this land to the land he swore to Abraham, to Isaac, and to Jacob. When the time comes for you to return to take the Promised Land, take my bones with you."[12]

Jacob's sons talked about the land of their fathers often, but it was hard to imagine anyone actually leaving Goshen. Bodies at rest tend to stay at rest. But return they would, and all it would take to set them on the road back to Canaan would be a regime change.

The pharaoh died and Egypt found a new king, one who didn't know Joseph. He said to his people, "Look at them. The people of Israel are too many. Our economy needs them, but if they ever decided to rise up against me, they would be too mighty to control. We need to deal shrewdly with them, lest they multiply even more and decide go to war, or worse, leave."

So the new king set taskmasters over them and made them slaves.[13] Generations before any of this took place, the Lord had told their great-grandfather, Abraham, "Know this. Your offspring will sojourn in a land that is not theirs, and they will be slaves there, afflicted for four hundred years."[14]

---

[11] JN 10:10   [13] EX 1:8–11
[12] GEN 50:24–25   [14] GEN 15:13–14

Now they were living out his words. This slavery would last for four centuries. During those years, they would multiply even as that first generation who came in under Joseph's protection died out completely. Four hundred years was enough time to convince the people they were meant to be slaves of Egypt.

But this was not who they were. Late in the evening when the workday was done, the parents settled in around the fire and told their children the old, old stories of the generations before. The kids imagined the red-headed Esau with his beard in a bowl of stew. Or giggled at the thought of Jacob staring, undone by the beauty of Rachel. Or shuddered at the image of Abraham raising his knife over Isaac's chest. Though they'd heard that story a thousand times, they still prayed that God would spare him, every time.

The children could sense in their parents that these were more than stories from the past. They were somehow still connected to the present and pushing forward to the future. From the stories, it seemed like the God of their fathers used to appear to them on a regular basis. He used to shake the earth. He even wrestled with Jacob on the banks of the Jabbok, wherever that was.

And all of this, they were told, was because God had promised to take Abraham's descendants as his people—to love them with an everlasting love and to never, ever leave them.

So where had he gone? Where was he now?

9

PASS OVER US

EXODUS 12:1–12

EAR THE END of those four hundred years, for reasons other than political upheaval or Egypt's economy or famine or war, the Lord called another servant from among his people—this one ironically of the house of Pharaoh himself. Born of parents from the house of Levi, Jacob's third son by Leah, Moses came into this world at a time when the new pharaoh was trying to curb Israel's population by killing their newborn sons. To save his life, Moses' mother hid him in a basket and had his sister float him downriver to where Pharaoh's daughter would bathe.

Pharaoh's daughter found the baby boy and wanted to take him home as her own. Seeing that she was drawn to little Moses, his sister came out of hiding to ask if the princess would like for her to find a nurse from among the Hebrew women to help care for the child. The princess did, so Moses' sister ran to tell their mother what had happened, and this was how Moses' mother joined Pharaoh's staff as a nurse to her own son—and how a little

Levite boy came to be the surrogate grandson of the king of Egypt.[1]

Moses grew up as one of the royal family's own sons. All the wealth, provisions, and education of the rich and powerful empire of Egypt were his—making him one of the most privileged children in the entire world. But just outside his palace, in the slave camps that dotted the plains of the Nile, lived the Hebrews, his true family. Much of the wealth and comforts afforded to Moses every day of his life came through the brutal oppression of his cousins, uncles, brothers, and sisters.

As Moses grew older, his awareness of this reality also grew, and so did the conflict within. Though he moved with all the freedom of the grandson of the king among the herds, fields, quarries, and building sites in Egypt, they teemed with his enslaved relatives, who were giving their lives to make their oppressor stronger. It was unjust, and he knew it.

One day, as a young man, Moses saw an Egyptian guard beating a Hebrew slave. Compelled to help one of his own people, Moses ran to help the slave, killing the guard. But this didn't garner the respect he hoped for from the Hebrews, which left Moses in a precarious place. To his own people, he was a defector from birth, and now to the house of Pharaoh, he was a murderer of Egyptians. Killing that guard made Moses a man without a home. It sent him into exile to escape death at the hands of the king's soldiers.[2]

During those many days, the king of Egypt died, and the people of Israel groaned because of their slavery and cried out for help. God heard their groaning, and God remembered his covenant with Abraham, with Isaac, and

---

[1] Ex 2:1–10   [2] Ex 2:11–15

with Jacob.[3] So the Lord called Moses out of exile to return to Goshen to lead Israel out of their slavery and bondage. Moses knew this would present two considerable obstacles—first, getting his own people to listen to this Levite of the house of Pharaoh, and second, getting Pharaoh to listen to this murderous traitor of the house of Levi.

As for his own people, the Lord said, "Gather the elders of Israel and say, 'The God of your fathers, Abraham, Isaac, and Jacob, appeared to me, saying, "I have seen what has been done to you in Egypt, and I promise to bring you out of the affliction of Egypt to the Promised Land flowing with milk and honey."' They will listen to your voice."[4]

Pharaoh was another matter. Israel represented a large and inexpensive work force. There was no way he would release them willingly, so God peeled back Pharaoh's hold on them one finger at a time by sending ten plagues upon the land. Pharaoh's heart was hard, and the first nine couldn't move it.[5] So the last plague was the worst: the death of the firstborn sons.

But the Lord gave Moses a word for Israel. He told them their firstborn sons would live to see another day if they put the blood of a lamb on their door posts when death passed through the land.[6] The image was clear and haunting. The angel of death would see blood glistening on the doorpost and count it as a sign that blood had already been shed in that home—that the people in that house had already surrendered to God what the angel had come to collect. Just as the Lord accepted the life of the ram in the thicket in the place of Abraham's son Isaac, so now God

---

[3] Ex 2:23–25   [5] Ex 7–10
[4] Ex 3:16–18   [6] Ex 12:13

accepted the blood of an innocent lamb for the blood of the sons of Abraham's descendants—a life for a life.

The lambs were led to the slaughter, and their blood covered the doorposts of the homes of the people of God. And when death passed through the land that night, the firstborn sons of Israel were spared while the firstborn sons of Egypt were not. Though the descendants of Jacob were certainly relieved, this was still a tragic night for everyone—sad for the memories of lifetimes of oppression, sad for the warring nature of this broken world, and sad for all the dead in Egypt.

God told Israel never to forget this moment. It wasn't just that he was liberating them from bondage. It was what he was delivering them *to*—the land the Lord had sworn to give them. But it was so much more than that. This night when God passed over the homes adorned with the blood of a lamb, he ratified his promise that he was taking these descendants of Abraham somewhere—that after over one hundred years of their forefathers' wanderings followed by another four hundred years of slavery, God had not forgotten his people. These people were "a people holy to the Lord their God. The Lord their God chose them as a people for his treasured possession, out of all peoples who are on the face of the earth."[7]

So the people of God grew up with the command to tell this story—the story of the rebellion in the Garden, the devastation of the flood, the wanderings of the patriarchs and the covenant promises God cut with them, the four hundred years in bondage to Egypt, and God's holy and sober deliverance that followed. What was the point? God had claimed a people as his own, a people he swore to

---

[7] Dt 7:6

one day fully redeem and fully restore. This wasn't a simple matter of the Divine helping his subjects when they got into scrapes. This was a matter of affection, of adoption, of redemption, and of a salvation belonging, from beginning to end, to the Lord.[8]

It had been hard, waiting those four hundred years, fighting back the fear that God had forgotten them. It would have been easy to reduce every facet of their existence down to one thing: getting out of Egypt. How easy it would have been to forget that God's covenant wasn't just about what he would deliver them from. His promise wasn't only a call out of bondage, though it was that. It was a call to Someone. God's call on the lives of his people has always been, above all else, a call to himself. He set his affection on his people and promised to make them clean and to give them life.

But the Lord also made it clear from the start that since the wages of sin is death, being reconciled to him would be a bloody business.[9] He accepted the blood of another in their place—a ram for Isaac, lambs for the firstborn sons of Israel, and later he would establish an entire system by which the people could offer sacrifices to God to atone for their sins.

But this system was unending—a reality that even worked its way into the design of their tabernacle. When Israel built her first temple many years later, there was no chair for the priest because his work was never done. The line of sacrificial lambs seemed to stretch on forever because no beast of the field could ever be perfect enough to actually take away the sins of the image bearers of God. Would there ever come a perfect, lasting, atoning sacrifice—one

---

[8] JONAH 2:9   [9] GEN 2:17, ROM 6:23

who could take away the sins of the world? If so, that lamb would have to be divine.

The Passover brought Egypt to her knees. Devastated, Pharaoh sent the people of Israel away. For the next forty years, Moses led his people. He didn't just lead them out of Egypt, he led them in the ways of following the Lord. He led them through the Red Sea on dry ground—an act the Lord used to establish Moses' leadership for the years to come.[10] And he led them through the first reading of the Law of the Lord, inscribed in stone by the very finger of God, which he brought down from Sinai.[11] The Lord spoke with Moses, who spoke to the people. And the people spoke to Moses, who spoke with the Lord.[12]

Still, for all Moses' greatness, from the day God sent him to lead, the people complained about him. This wasn't because Moses was a bad leader, but because in order for people to be led, they must leave something behind— and people grow fond of home, even if they've only been enslaved there. For every step Moses led them to freedom, they found something to lament and complain about.

In the desert, the people had nothing to drink. They grumbled that they would have given anything for the grapes and pomegranates and figs of Egypt. "Why did you bring us up out of Egypt to this evil place?" they said to Moses.[13] Moses took their complaint to the Lord, who told him to take his staff to a rock in the camp and, in the presence of the people, he was to tell it to yield its water, and it would.[14] They wanted grape juice and pomegranate

---

[10] Ex 14–15   [12] Ex 20:19   [14] Num 20:8
[11] Ex 19–20   [13] Num 20:5

nectar, but God essentially told them, as parents have down through the ages, "I'll get you a drink of water."

But Moses had had enough. He gathered the people, chastised them for their rebellious hearts, and then walked over to the rock, raised his staff, and struck it in anger before their eyes. Water poured out, but Moses had sinned. He struck when only words were needed, and this act betrayed his anger not only toward the people, but toward God.

The rock and the water that would miraculously flow from it were God's handiwork and under his control. The man who struck the rock wanted to strike God. God knew it. Moses knew it.

God's discipline was that Moses wouldn't be the one to lead the people into the land. Moses, the one God called to lead the people out of Egypt, the one who led them across the dry ground that only moments before had been the Red Sea, the man who carried down from Mt. Sinai the Ten Commandments, would not see this journey to its end.

The truth was that Moses' life spanned only a small part of the story he was in. He was a player in the drama of the promise of redemption God had made hundreds of years before he came on the scene.[15] Though this was difficult for Moses, the Lord's discipline held an important truth for all who would be called upon to lead his people: Moses wasn't meant to be the hero of Israel's story. Someone else was.

---

[15] Dt 34:4

10

---~~~---

The War Within

 SMALL TEAM OF spies crept up the southern ridge of the Negev. On the other side lay what Moses had sent them to observe—the land of Canaan and its inhabitants. It would be a dangerous mission, but they wanted to know what lay ahead when the time came to inherit the Promised Land. The plan was to blend in with the Canaanites, explore as much of the land as they could, and return with a report.

As for the bounty the land had to offer, they had never seen anything like it. The vineyards produced clusters of grapes so big it took two people to carry them.[1] It was a verdant land flowing with milk and honey. Compared to the desert they'd been wandering in all this time, it was hard to imagine such abundance.

But the inhabitants of the land matched its bounty. They were bigger than anyone the spies had ever seen. It was hard to imagine how the weary clans of displaced

---

[1] Num 13:23

65

slaves in the southern desert could overcome the giants in the land of Canaan. It was an impossible task.

When the spies returned to give their report, a few stepped forward to speak for the group. "The land is the richest, most abundant place we've ever seen. But the people who live there are so big they made us feel like grasshoppers. We can't overtake them."[2]

But two of the spies, Joshua and Caleb, stepped forward in protest. They were incensed at this faithless fear. This wasn't about whether the Hebrew people could overcome the Canaanites. This was about what God was going to do. The land was not theirs to take. It was God's to give to them. It shouldn't matter if the inhabitants were as tall as cedars. God had promised this land to their fathers, and God would give it to them.[3]

Caleb continued, "This is God's fight. I say we go and take it now."

But the others rebuked him. It would be a death march, they insisted. When the rest of Israel heard them argue, their faith also drained away, and they wept in despair. "It would have been better for us to die in Egypt! Why is God bringing us out here to die by the sword?"[4]

Joshua protested, "It's a good land. A really good land. If God delights in us, he'll give it to us. To run away now is to rebel against him. Don't do it."[5]

But fear had so gripped the people that their hearts were stuck.

Joshua was right. The Lord received their lack of faith as rebellion against him and told Moses that because they didn't believe he could lead them into the land, he wouldn't.

---

[2] Num 13:31–33   [4] Num 14:2–3
[3] Num 13:30–33   [5] Num 14:7–9

Every last person in their generation except Joshua and Caleb would die in the desert, leaving the inheritance of the Promised Land to the next generation.

God's promise to Abraham long ago was magnificent. He swore to them that they would be a great nation and they would be a blessed nation.[6] The Lord had made them into a great nation, but they did not feel blessed. They felt tired. Their story was of a people either sojourning as strangers in strange lands or living and dying as slaves in the service of men who didn't care to know their God. But surely God knew their weariness. Surely he knew what they needed. More than anything in the world, the people longed for rest.

Rest.

But now the reality was setting in that in order for them to find rest—rest from their wanderings, rest from their slavery, rest from the Lord's discipline, rest from the wars within and the wars without—they first had to overcome. And the land was as the spies described it, teeming with strong warriors fueled by the fiercest motive any fighting men have ever known—protecting their homes.

There was no way around it. There would be no home without a conquest.

ISRAEL REMAINED IN the wilderness until the last of the faithless generation had died. There were battles along the way, and the Lord bolstered the faith of the next generation by giving them miraculous victories over Edom and Moab.

When the time came for Israel to enter the Promised Land, an old and dying Moses led them to the eastern banks of the Jordan River. His death and burial was one of

[6] GEN 12:2

the most beautiful and sacred moments in history.[7] Before he died, he passed his mantle of leadership on to Joshua.[8]

Moses had led the people like a shepherd—caring for their needs, showing them the way, rescuing them from pits and wolves. Joshua's leadership would be different. He would lead them as a warrior. The Lord told him, "As I was with Moses, so I am with you. Do not be afraid. I go before you."[9]

Their first steps of conquest were not a battle, but a river crossing. And there, to remind the people that he was the same God who led them out of Egypt, the Lord parted the waters of the Jordan so that they could cross into the Promised Land in the same way their parents passed through the Red Sea and left their slavery behind—on dry ground. As they crossed the river, they pulled up stones covered for years in the Jordan to make a memorial to stand as a testimony to the Lord's faithfulness.

The time had come to take the land, and Joshua was confident in his Captain's command. To him, the men of Israel were no longer slaves. They were soldiers. He would lead them through the valleys of the shadows of their fears. He would teach them the cadence of the Lord marching out before them. He would lead them up from the Jordan to the clearing where their first objective, standing like a pillar of sand and stone, would come into view: Jericho.

In a way, Jericho represented the entire conquest. To take any of the land, they would have to start with Jericho. And if the Lord gave them Jericho, what couldn't they take? But God would have to be the one to do this.

And he did. The way the Lord delivered Jericho to Israel stunned the world. The news of Israel's victory instilled in

---

[7] Dt 34   [8] Dt 31   [9] Josh 1:5

the neighboring cities a fear of not only the Hebrew people, but also of their commander Joshua, who seemed to have the power of God behind him. The confidence of Joshua's army lay in the strength of the Lord, and they swept through the land as one city after another fell.

When the conquest was complete, Joshua assembled the people. They had some unfinished business with the Lord. As great as their victories had been, there was still another war to fight, one that had been raging since long before any of them could remember. It was a war against God—a siren song calling the hearts of every man to reject the Lord and serve other gods who could be tamed, placated, or bargained with. Men could conquer the world and still be stuck in the mire of this fight.

The Lord had promised to give this land to the children of Abraham, and now it was theirs. He had loved them with an enduring love. Joshua reminded them of the road they'd walked—of their history as nomads and slaves, of the Red Sea and the Jordan. The Lord had been faithful to them.[10]

But Joshua also reminded them that for their part, they had not been faithful. They had forsaken the Lord more times than any of them cared to remember. They had sought after the gods of the nations around them,[11] and when those were not available, they made gods of their own.[12] Now the stakes were higher than ever. If Israel turned to worshiping other gods, the Lord would cut them off from this land.[13]

"You will be tempted to turn to other gods. Choose this day whom you will serve."[14]

---

[10] JOSH 24   [12] EX 32   [14] JOSH 24:15
[11] JOSH 7:10–26   [13] JOSH 23:16

The people insisted, "We will serve the Lord and him only."[15]

Joshua answered, "But you're not able. You know this. God is holy, but time and time again you forsake him for idols. Know this: when you do, he will judge you for it."[16]

But they insisted, "We mean it. We will follow the Lord. We will obey his voice."[17]

So Joshua told the people to set up another memorial, only this one wasn't meant to serve as a testimony to the faithfulness of God. This one was meant to stand as a witness against them if they ever abandoned their promise.[18]

Their hearts so longed for rest, and the Lord had given it. They were home. They couldn't fathom ever taking the Lord's mercy and kindness for granted. But Joshua's warning was plain. Their peace would depend on their ability to follow the Lord and serve him only. This was a position of tenuous rest. It could be lost so easily.

Joshua, the commander of the Lord's army, had led the people into the land of their inheritance. But their security there balanced on the fulcrum of their obedience. Tip either way—to godlessness or to the worship of many gods—and the Lord would cut them off from the land of their inheritance. There would be an edge even to their rest.

There was only so much Joshua could do for them. He could warn them. He could remind them of their past history with idolatry. He could take them through the stories of the generations before, who had, without exception, at one point or another embraced the gods of their neighboring countries. He could implore, threaten, pray, and appeal. He could pound his fists on his pulpit. He could

---

[15] JOSH 24:21
[16] JOSH 24:19–21
[17] JOSH 24:24
[18] JOSH 24:26–27

plead from his knees. He could sing in the sweetest whisper of a lullaby.

But one thing he could not do. He could not make them holy. He could warn them of their proclivity to sin, but he could not take it from them. He could vividly predict their certain coming guilt, but he could not remove it. He could lead many of the sons of Israel to consider their place in this world, but he could not lead any sons to glory.[19]

---

[19] HEB 2:9–10

11

TWELVE TRIBES AND
NO CROWN

JUDGES 2:16–23

N THOSE DAYS Israel had no king, and everyone did what was right in his or her own eyes.[1] What looked right to many was the opulence and sensuality of the Canaanite religion, so before long the children of Abraham ran to the arms of foreign gods. The covenant promises Israel rehearsed and handed down through the generations included the promise that they would become a great nation. For many, when they looked at the temples and gold and women of Canaan, they thought they were seeing greatness.

The temptation to follow the gods of Canaan was strong. Their religion was raw and brutal, with a certain logic that appealed to these people whose history was so saddled with the ongoing need to put their faith in the God of their fathers.[2]

Though Baal, Ashtoreth and the other gods in Canaan sometimes elicited unspeakable brutality from their devotees—like self-mutilation and human sacrifice—they

---

[1] JDG 17:6   [2] PHIL 4:19

could be appeased through offerings. Baal, who was said to rule the thunder and rain, could give the people abundant harvest, though he could also wilt them under a drought. Ashtoreth was believed to oversee human fertility, and she could either give or withhold from the people the most valuable commodity in the world: children to help perform the labor the family needed for their survival.

The economy of the Canaanite religion eliminated the need for faith—and that sparkled with an irresistible brilliance, perhaps even more than their temples adorned with gold or their women adorned with precious stones. It seemed so simple. All they had to do was give in order to get. So the children of Israel turned from the ways of their fathers, who obeyed the commands of the Lord. They followed after other gods and bowed down to them.[3]

When God's people gave in to the temptation to worship other gods, their idolatry sent their national and spiritual life into a downward spiral of apostasy and chaos. The cycle that developed looked like this: The people rejected the Lord and worshiped other gods, so the Lord allowed them to be conquered and oppressed by the nations whose gods they worshipped. Crushed under this oppression, Israel cried out to the Lord for help, and the Lord sent a deliverer to rescue them. (These deliverers were called judges.) With each judge, the delivered people returned to the Lord for a time, serving him only. But eventually they turned again to foreign gods and the cycle started over, under a deeper oppression than the one before.

First there was Caleb's nephew, Othniel of Judah. When the people of Israel began to worship Baal, the Lord mobilized the Mesopotamian army to crush them.

---

[3] JDG 2:17

For eight long years Israel suffered under Mesopotamia, until the Lord called Othniel to lead Israel in battle. The Lord gave them victory over their enemies, and the people enjoyed forty years of peace.[4]

But Othniel died, and the people returned to their idolatry. So God raised up Eglon, the fat King of Moab, who brought another eighteen years of oppression to God's people. The people cried out for mercy, and God gave them Ehud of Benjamin, who killed Eglon. The people enjoyed eighty years of peace under Ehud, but eventually he died, and with him died his vision for righteousness. The people again did evil in the eyes of the Lord.[5]

After that came Jabin, King of Canaan, and with him, war. He oppressed the people for twenty years before they cried out for relief. This time God gave them Deborah of Ephraim, who led Israel's generals in campaigns that left Israel awestruck by her resolve. Deborah led Israel to another forty years of peace.[6]

But the people turned yet again to idols. This time it was the Midianites who brought war. They subdued Israel for seven years, until the people again prayed for mercy and the Lord gave them Gideon. Gideon was strong and brave, but he was also a man of faltering faith. He destroyed the idols of foreign gods wherever he found them, but he struggled to trust the God who called him. Still, he brought Israel four decades of peace until they again turned to idols.[7]

Jephthah of Gilead-Manasseh came after Gideon. After twenty-four years of oppression at the hands of the Ammonites, Jephthah led Israel to twenty-four years of peace.[8] But

---

[4] JDG 3:7–11 [6] JDG 4–5 [8] JDG 10:6–12:7
[5] JDG 3:12–30 [7] JDG 7:2–8

he tended to let his power go to his head. He trusted the authority of his own word over the word of God—a tragic flaw that cost his daughter her life.[9]

Predictably, the people again turned away from the Lord. This time the Lord sent the Philistines, who brought another forty years of oppression. The people cried out, and the Lord sent Samson of the tribe of Dan. Physically, Samson was the strongest man anyone had ever known. But his character was weak, and though he could subdue armies, he couldn't subdue his own appetite for women or his thirst for drinking.[10] Samson led Israel to twenty years of peace.[11]

There were other judges as well. All told, this cycle of oppression and relief occupied more than four hundred of Israel's first five hundred years in the Promised Land, which was more than enough time for them to get used to an existence of idolatry, war, and desperation. But there was also enough time between oppressions for the people to believe that next time things would be different. They would learn from their mistakes, and their new judge would learn from the flaws of his predecessor. In their minds, each new judge held the potential to give them what the previous judge could not—lasting peace.

But each of the judges shared a fundamental problem: They were deeply flawed and often faithless people, just like the people they led. With each judge things seemed to improve, but when the people again rebelled against the Lord, they fell even further. They faced a cold reality. The core of their problem wasn't that neighboring kings kept attacking them and prevailing. It was that they were an unfaithful people.

---

[9] JDG 11:29–40   [10] JDG 14:10, 16:1   [11] JDG 13–16

They were crooked deep down. The people had led themselves away from God. The judges often acted heroically, but they couldn't save anyone. Israel looked to their heroes for so much, but as long as God's people were led by ordinary men, they would be led by men with flaws. Whatever bounty these flawed leaders might deliver, it would always come mixed with a bitter fruit; the judges could lead the people out of external trouble, but they couldn't lead them to true repentance. They could subdue an entire army but not a single heart.

Still, Israel remained a people with a strong sense of national identity. They were people of a common law—the Law of God. They were no more or less fickle than any of the God-fearing people who came before them or after. They were a people who needed to return again and again to the truth of who they were. They needed to hear that the Lord their God was one. They needed to remember that the most authentic way for them to live as his people was to love him with everything they had and were, and to love their neighbors as they loved themselves. They needed to know that in the law of the Lord lay their freedom as a nation.

But they couldn't cling to these truths on their own, and because they couldn't, they were a people of great sorrow, acquainted with grief.[12] The cycle of their idolatry never once gave them any joy or purpose or satisfaction. Only pain. And with the pain came discipline. But behind the discipline there was love.[13]

The pain of this downward cycle was not something God manufactured as a means of discipline. The pain was simply the fruit of every man doing what was right in his

---

[12] Isa 53:3   [13] Prov 13:24, Heb 12:6

own eyes—nothing more, nothing less. God didn't need to manufacture punishment to awaken them to their sin. The natural consequence of their sin of rejecting him brought a world of pain all its own. Their sin was, in itself, a form of discipline. Every day spent worrying about the lack of rain was a worry-filled day the people couldn't take back. Every dalliance with temple prostitutes eroded away layers of trust their marriages would struggle to regain.

When the people turned away to worship other gods, they trained their hearts to no longer hope or pray or trust or delight in being known by the God who held their fate. The God of Abraham was living and glorious, and his worshippers were being conformed to his image.[14] Baal and Ashtoreth, on the other hand, were lifeless stone. Still, their followers also slowly took on *their* likenesses—beginning with a coldness in their hearts that worked its way out toward their communities. This was the fruit of worship— that worshippers came to resemble the object of their adoration. For Israel, this was leading some to glory—but it was leading many others to ruin.[15]

Nevertheless, during this season of Israel's development, even in all their unfaithfulness, the Lord remained faithful to them. Even though all Israel fell away from God, God didn't abandon them. There was a bitter edge to this mercy since Israel's sin—their returning again and again to idolatry—was a rejection of the Lord himself. They were saying to him as clearly as they could, "You're not the God we want."

But these were the people he wanted, so he continually rescued them from the trouble they brought upon themselves.

---

[14] ROM 8:29   [15] EZK 6:6, HEB 2:10

In those days, Israel was twelve tribes with no crown. They needed a king to lead them. A godly king. They didn't need a king to help them amass wealth or conquer other nations. They needed a king who would fight to return them over and over again to the heart of God's law. Israel needed a king whose sole passion was to do the will of the One who sent him,[16] someone who would lead God's people in righteousness.

Israel needed a perfect king.[17] They were called to love the Lord their God with all their heart, soul, and strength and to live as his children, loved with an everlasting love. But without a king to lead them, they would only do what seemed right in their own eyes.

They needed a king to govern their hearts.

---

[16] Jn 4:34   [17] Jdg 21:25

12

A KING ON A THRONE

1 SAMUEL 8:1–22

HE PRIEST NOTICED Hannah when she arrived. Her husband, Elkanah, had gone to present his offering to the Lord while Hannah stayed behind. Coming to the tabernacle always seemed to stir the deep waters of her heart. Today was one of those days.

She thanked God for her husband. He was a decent man who treated her like a treasure. But she wondered what value she really held. Though she'd been trying through their entire marriage, she couldn't conceive. More than anything, she wanted a son. She wept when she thought about it. When Elkanah saw her weeping, it hurt his heart too. "Sweet Hannah, why is your heart sad? Am I not worth more to you than ten sons?"[1] She loved him, but this ache in her heart came from a place he'd never be able to comfort.

Eli the priest watched her from the doorway. Hannah's shoulders rose and fell to the rhythm of her breathing. She

---

[1] 1 SAM 1:8

looked elegant and beautiful kneeling there with her hair hanging over her face. But then he noticed her lips moving, as if she was talking to herself. Suddenly she looked more like the shuffling cast-offs who drank their way through the afternoon in the streets, mumbling in private conversations with the spirits they consumed.

Eli confronted her. "Is this what you've become? A drunk?"[2]

She looked up at him, eyes swollen with tears. "I'm not drunk," she said. "I'm pouring out my soul before the Lord." She told Eli about her longing for a son, and Eli prayed that the Lord would give her one.

The Lord did. She named the boy Samuel.

Hannah and Elkanah knew their son was a gift from the Lord, and they agreed to give the boy back to him. As soon as he was old enough, he would go live with the priests and grow up in a life of blessing and service to the Lord and his people.

Samuel grew in wisdom and faith, and when he became a man, the Lord called him to serve as the final judge for Israel. He would serve as a prophet, priest, and judge, since in those days Israel had no king.

But they wanted a king. They looked at the nations around them, saw their kings, and wanted to be like them. They went to Samuel and asked for a different leader.

It was hard for Samuel to hear them reject him as their leader, but the Lord told him, "They aren't rejecting you, Samuel. I'm the one they're rejecting. From the day I brought them out of the land of Egypt, they have forsaken me for other gods, and now they're doing it again. I'm going to give them a king, Samuel. But I want you to warn them about what comes with such power in the hands of a man."[3]

Samuel gathered the people and told them, "God is going to give you a king. But know this: your king will rule over you. He'll make you farm his land while he taxes you for your crops and vineyards. He'll take the best of your fields, livestock, and women and use them to build his kingdom. He'll send your sons off to war and your daughters off to make clothing and perfume. You'll become slaves again, and you'll cry out to the Lord for help. Again. But this time God won't deliver you. Is this really what you want?"[4]

The people answered, "It is. We want to be like the nations around us. We want a king on a throne, full of power, with a sword in his fist—someone to rule us, fight for us, and establish us."[5]

It might have occurred to Samuel that perhaps one of his own sons could succeed him, were it not for the sad fact that they didn't appear to be following in his footsteps.[6] He didn't presume that the Lord meant to call one of his sons to rule over Israel, so he asked the Lord to lead him to the one who would.

There was a wealthy man from the tribe of Benjamin named Kish, and Kish had a son named Saul. As a young man, Saul carried himself as someone who considered the burdens of his community to be his own. He was fair-minded, well-spoken, and responsible.[7] Saul was also rich, tall, and handsome, more attractive than anyone the women in his hometown had ever seen.[8] The Lord arranged for Samuel and Saul to meet. Samuel knew he was looking at Israel's future king.

---

[3] 1 SAM 8:7–9   [5] 1 SAM 8:19–20   [7] 1 SAM 9:3–26
[4] 1 SAM 8:11–18   [6] 1 SAM 2:12   [8] 1 SAM 9:1–2

Samuel prophesied over Saul that he was Israel's prince—God's anointed king: "The Spirit of the Lord will come upon you and when you speak to your people, the Lord will go before you and he will give you another heart. He will transform you into a different man."[9] For all the apparent greatness of Saul, the king the Lord would make of him required more than Saul's inherent strengths. The Lord would have to give him what he needed to become the leader God was calling him to be.

In his early days Saul wore the crown well. Israel was energized by the newness of their perceived position of strength. Little by little, Saul accomplished more and more, establishing himself as an effective and reliable leader. He was resolute in leadership and fearsome in battle, but this would be tested.

The Philistines gathered for war—thirty thousand chariots, six thousand horsemen, and troops more numerous than the sand on the seashore. They took up posts surrounding the western communities of Israel, and Saul's people knew they were in trouble. Their fear became so great that many ran and, ironically, hid in their own forebears' tombs.[10]

The king prepared for battle. He gathered his troops like the warrior he was. But Saul wanted to take his preparations even further by having Samuel offer sacrifices to the Lord on their behalf in the hope that God would give them victory. The king waited and waited for his priest to arrive, but Samuel didn't come.

Only God's appointed priests were allowed to offer these sacrifices to the Lord, but with every passing day, Saul could tell that the hearts of his already nervous troops' were beginning to falter.[11] So the king made a judgment call: "Bring the offerings to me. I'll present them to the Lord."

---

[9] 1 Sam 10:6–9   [10] 1 Sam 13:2–7   [11] 1 Sam 13:8

With the blood of the sacrifices still wet on Saul's hands, Samuel arrived. "Saul, what have you done?"

"You said you were coming, but you never came. Meanwhile I've been watching the courage drain from my soldiers' hearts while the Philistine garrison continued to swell. This war is coming, and I don't want to go into battle without the Lord's blessing."[12]

Saul had been given so much, but he made the grave mistake of thinking that what he possessed had come to him by his own hand. He thought that what Israel needed was something he could give. He thought they needed his strength, his wisdom, and his righteousness. And he believed he could give these to them.

But he didn't recognize that he treated the God of his fathers like any other god. When he saw his troops arrayed before him, he counted them up and doubted that they would be able to defeat the Philistines, as if the outcome of this battle hinged on the size of his army. He believed he needed his God's blessing, just as the Philistines believed they needed the blessings of theirs, so he brought an offering, hoping to rally the Lord behind him, just as the Philistines had done with their gods.

Saul presumed that since he was the king, he could also do the work of a priest, even though the prophet had forbidden it. This wasn't just a mistake. It was an offense to a holy God who swore that he wouldn't give his glory to another.[13] Saul was not God's peer, nor was he made righteous by his crown. The priests were consecrated to act as mediators between a holy God and sinful humanity. They offered sacrifices to atone for their own sins just to be able to bring offerings on behalf of others.[14] Their work among

---

[12] 1 SAM 13:11–12   [13] ISA 48:11   [14] HEB 7:27

the people was holy, bloody, and humbling. God was not like them, and they were not like God.

There lay a chasm between God and his people that ran as deep as the sin in the hearts of men. It was one thing if their holy God deigned to grace them with his presence, but it was another thing entirely for one of his people to presume that they held the right to ascend to his holy throne. Saul thought he could bend the providence of God around the persuasion of his sacrifices, even though he had never been anointed to act as his people's priest.

Saul's presumption was a foreshadowing of how he would become everything the Lord warned his people about. Any king who thinks he commands the God who appointed him to rule will come to regard himself as the Lord over his people, as though they belong to him.

With his sacrifice, Saul rejected the Lord. And when he did it, the Lord rejected him as king.

Samuel's voice cracked as tears gathered in the corners of his eyes. He said, "You've done a foolish thing, king, counting yourself as a priest. You've disobeyed God's commands. Had you kept them, he would have established your throne forever. But I'm telling you now that this kingdom of yours will not continue. The Lord will give his people another king—a man after his own heart, which you are not."[15]

After that, things were never the same between Samuel and Saul. Every time Samuel looked at Israel's first earthly king, he knew he was looking at the second of her kings to be rejected—the first being the Lord himself. He knew Saul wouldn't leave his throne willingly. Saul vacillated between defiance and repentance, pleading with Samuel for forgiveness[16] and then threatening to kill him.[17]

---

[15] I SAM 13:13–14   [16] I SAM 15:24   [17] I SAM 15:27

Samuel grieved over Saul. He struggled with his own culpability in the king's collapse. Could he have done a better job training him in the ways of God?

The Lord said to Samuel, "How long will you grieve over Saul? I have rejected him as king over Israel. That's done. Fill your horn with oil and go. I'm sending you to visit a man named Jesse in Bethlehem. I have provided for myself a king from among his sons."[18]

And then the Lord reminded him of a truth that led to Saul's downfall but would restore Samuel's confidence. "Do not look for the strongest or most attractive. I do not see as man sees: man looks at the outward appearance, but I look on the heart."[19]

---

[18] 1 Sam 16:1   [19] 1 Sam 16:7

13

THE BOY-KING OF BETHLEHEM

2 SAMUEL 7:1–29

ITH THE LIGHT of the Lord's instruction leading him, Samuel rode into Bethlehem looking for a king. He found Jesse, who introduced him to the rest of his family. One by one Jesse brought his sons before Samuel, and one by one Samuel asked the Lord if he was looking at Israel's next king.

Jesse's sons were strong. Any one of them would have made a fine king if appearance was all that mattered. But the Lord had told Samuel not to judge them by their appearance. What God cared about most was the heart. Seven sons passed before Samuel, and seven times the Lord told him, "This is not the king."[1]

Samuel was confused. "Are all your sons here?"

Jesse said, "I have another son, the youngest. He's out shepherding in the fields."

"Please go get him."

David walked in from the fields, ruddy, with striking eyes.[2] As soon as Samuel saw him, the Lord told him, "This

---

[1] 1 Sam 16:9   [2] 1 Sam 16:12

is the one. Arise and anoint him." In front of Jesse and
David's older brothers, Samuel anointed the boy's head
with the oil he had brought, and when he did, the Spirit of
the Lord came upon David and stayed with him from that
day forward.[3]

Soon after this discrete ceremony, Jesse took David to
the house of Saul, where David became one of the king's
servants. Saul grew to love David. He made David his
armor-bearer, which kept David closer to the king than
most.

The Lord had already rejected Saul as king. He had
taken his Holy Spirit from him, and from then on, Saul
wrestled with inner demons as he tried to cobble together
the best kingdom he could build. His inner turmoil often
drove him to the edge of madness. When it did, David
played the lyre, calming the king's heart with song.[4]

SKIRMISHES WITH THE Philistines were threatening to turn
into all-out war, and down in the valley of Elah, Saul's
forces had dug in to one side while the Philistines held the
other. Every day the Philistines' best warrior, a giant of a
man named Goliath, taunted Saul's army, "Why don't you
send your champion down into the valley, and he and I can
settle this man to man?"

Israel did have a champion, but he was just as afraid as
the rest of his men.[5] Their champion was Saul, their commander and king.

Some of David's brothers were among Saul's forces,
and Jesse sent David to bring them supplies and see about
their well-being. Not long after David arrived, Goliath
came out, again taunting Israel's army.

[3] I SAM 16:13   [4] I SAM 16:23   [5] I SAM 17:11

The young shepherd's heart burned. "Who is this uncircumcised Philistine that he should defy the armies of the living God?"[6] David believed it was God who ruled and kept Israel. He believed the Lord's hand was on them, hemming them in behind and before.[7]

So David looked around at the nervous warriors and said, "I'll fight him. And God will fight for me."[8]

But Saul wouldn't have it. David was no match for Goliath. Clearly. But David persisted until Saul relented, saying, "At least let me put my armor on you." The sad irony must have occurred to Saul that he, Israel's champion, was suiting up his armor-bearer to go and fight his battle.

But for David, this was never about whether or not he was a greater warrior than Saul. This was about a foul-mouthed Philistine defaming the name of his God. The armor didn't fit the boy, so he left it behind in exchange for five smooth stones and his sling. David understood that Goliath wasn't about to fight a boy. David was the providence of God standing before the giant.

When they met down by the Brook of Elah, David slung his stone straight and true, but it was the Lord who drove it squarely into the forehead of Goliath.

This was a moment that not only turned the tide of the war, but fixed the nation's attention on this brave shepherd-warrior. Saul took David into his house.[9] The king put the boy in charge of the troops, and David was victorious wherever he fought.

David was fast becoming famous. When he passed through the streets of a town, the people would come to get a look at him, and the women would sing songs of

---

[6] 1 SAM 17:26
[7] PS 139:5
[8] 1 SAM 17:37
[9] 1 SAM 18:2

adoration. "Saul has struck down his thousands and David his ten thousands!"[10]

Of course, this got under Saul's skin. David may have been a mighty warrior, but Saul was the king. The seeds of contempt found fertile soil, and they grew and grew until even the sight of David made the king want to kill him—a desire he attempted to satisfy on many occasions.[11]

David fought alongside men who developed a loyalty to him stronger than their loyalty to their king. These mighty men became David's friends and protectors. They were fearsome fighters willing to lay down their lives for their captain. Among David's mighty men was a man named Uriah the Hittite.[12]

Eventually Saul's commitment to kill David became so resolute that David had to go into hiding. His mighty men went with him. There were times when Saul got close enough to David that David's men wanted to take the fight to Saul and end it, but David wouldn't let them. Saul, for all his venom, was the king the Lord anointed over Israel. Who was David to depose God's anointed one?[13]

On one occasion, though, David and his men came closer to Saul than he could have dreamed. Saul had David and his men on the run. He took a break from his pursuit to relieve himself and ducked into the very cave where David and his men were hiding. David forbade his men to kill Saul, but he snuck over and cut off the corner of Saul's robe.

When Saul had finished, he stepped back out into the daylight, but from the mouth of the cave he heard, "My Lord the King!"

---

[10] I SAM 18:7   [12] 2 SAM 23:39
[11] I SAM 19:10, 20:33   [13] I SAM 24:1–7

Saul spun around. David emerged from the darkness with his men behind him.

David said, "These men wanted me to kill you, but I didn't. I spared you because even though you're trying to kill me, you're the Lord's anointed one, and I will not turn my hand against him. But I want you to know, my king, that it is my fidelity to the Lord that has spared your life today."[14]

With that, he held up the corner of Saul's robe. The king must have been speechless.

David continued, "I haven't sinned against you, have I? All I've ever done is serve you, and yet you hunt me like an enemy. The Lord will judge between us, king. I won't be your undoing. God will see to that. But as for me, I'm tired of this fight. I've asked the Lord to settle this. I've asked him to deliver me from your hand, just as he has delivered you from mine today."[15]

Saul stood there, humbled and stunned.

"David? David! You're more righteous than I. You have repaid my evil with mercy. You don't treat me like your enemy, though I am. Who finds his enemy and lets him get away? David, I know you're going to be king. I know you'll rule this kingdom better than I ever could. Please, I beg you. When you assume the throne, have mercy on my family. Spare them. Whatever happens between you and me, please spare them. Promise me."[16]

David promised Saul this mercy. His men watched the king register the vow like a glimmer of light that broke into his bleak and imminent future. They watched the king to see if he had anything to say, but he only looked at the ground, thinking. Without another word, he turned and walked away.

[14] 1 SAM 24:8–11   [15] 1 SAM 24:11–15   [16] 1 SAM 24:16–22

Though there remained plenty of fight in Saul, and though he didn't give up his pursuit to kill David, he knew that he had become David's new Goliath. He knew the story was already written. He knew he would fall. And he knew that this was never really a fight against David. What must have chilled him even more was that he knew *David* knew this. Saul's fight was with the Lord. David rested in that. Saul could not. For the rest of his days, he wrestled with this.

IN A LATER battle against the Philistines, Saul watched his army succumb to the advancing enemy. He watched his best soldiers fall. He watched as his sons were struck down on the fields of war. Before the Philistines had a chance to capture him, he took out his sword and fell on it, running himself through.[17]

When David heard about Saul's death, he mourned. He and his men settled in the towns of Hebron, and the leaders of the houses of Judah and Israel anointed David as their king.[18] David continued to lead his forces against Israel's enemies, and before long the Lord gave his people rest from war.[19]

There was a prophet in the land named Nathan. David sought Nathan's wisdom and counsel, and Nathan proved to be a man who heard the voice of the Lord. The Lord, through Nathan, said to David, "Do you remember how I took you out of the fields of your fathers? You were just a boy, a shepherd, and I made you a prince—Israel's young prince. David, I am working through you. I will make your name one of the greatest in history. I have been with you since the beginning of your days, and every victory you've

---

[17] I SAM 31:1–7   [18] 2 SAM 2:4, 5:3   [19] 2 SAM 7:1

ever had has come from my hand. There has been much war, but I will give you and your people rest. I'm making your kingdom into a place of peace."

Then the Lord continued through his prophet, "When you lie down with your fathers, David, I will raise up from among your offspring, from your own body, One who will establish his kingdom forever. He will build a house for my name and I will establish the throne of his kingdom forever. I will be his Father and he will be my Son—ancient and strong."[20]

David went to the house of the Lord and sat on the ground.[21] He prayed, "Who am I and what is my house that you would bring me this far? What can I say to you? You know my heart, Lord. Because of your promises to my fathers before me and according to what resides in your heart, you have brought about all this greatness that I might see it. There is no one like you. And who is like your people Israel, this one nation on earth you've chosen to redeem for yourself—a people to whom you'll give your own name?"[22]

For all the praise and glory David had received as Israel's hero over the years, he recognized in this encounter with God that every good thing in his life had come from the Lord. In this lucid moment, David saw that God's goodness to him was coming from a place deeper than he could imagine, and that it was in response to promises the Lord had made long before he was born.

To this David said, "May it please you to bless the house of your servant so that it *will* continue forever as you have spoken."[23]

---

[20] 2 Sam 7:8–14, Heb 1:5   [22] 2 Sam 7:18–28
[21] 2 Sam 7:18   [23] 2 Sam 7:28

14

DON'T GIVE UP
ON ME

PSALM 51

ARLY IN HIS reign David was a great king. He was courageous, wise, and decisive. He entrusted his battles to the Lord, never fearing when his enemies outnumbered the size of his army. He attracted loyal followers by the thousands. He came to embody Israel's idea of a great king to the extent that when people tried to imagine one greater, they tried to imagine someone more David-like than David himself.

But for all his greatness, David was also a man guided by his appetites. Late one afternoon, while his army was off fighting the Ammonites, David went up to his patio and saw a woman bathing on her roof. Her beauty overcame him, so he sent one of his messengers to get her. Her name was Bathsheba, and David took her into his bed.

Soon after that night she stood at the king's front door. "I'm pregnant."

David panicked, but his shame quickly gave way to planning. He told his servant, "Go get this woman's husband from the battle. Bring him home to his wife." David figured a short furlough for Bathsheba's husband would cause him to believe he was the father of the baby in his wife's belly.

Except that when Bathsheba's husband returned, he did not go to his house but to the palace. David tried to send him home, but the soldier had a long history with his king. His loyalty ran deep, and as long as they were at war, he would not leave his king for anything. David woke to find the man sleeping outside the front door of the palace where his wife had stood only weeks earlier.[1]

"Why didn't you go home to your wife?" David asked.

"My brothers are sleeping outside every night, fighting for you, my king. Who am I to take a night off from my solidarity with them or from my service to you? I won't do it."[2]

David tried again the next night to get this soldier to go home to his wife, this time plying him with alcohol. But the soldier wouldn't go. David realized there was a loyalty in this man he couldn't dissuade, so he sent him back to the front lines of battle and told his commanding officer to put him out where the fighting was the fiercest, and then to withdraw from him so that he might be struck down.

Bathsheba's husband was Uriah the Hittite, one of David's mighty men from his days of running from the madness of Saul.[3] Uriah was with David in the cave that day when they cut off the corner of Saul's robe. The two men had stood shoulder-to-shoulder many times in battle. Uriah wasn't just loyal to his country. He was loyal to the man who slept with his wife.

No doubt David had met Bathsheba before that fateful night. No doubt he had imagined what it was like for

---

[1] 2 SAM 11:6–10   [2] 2 SAM 11:11   [3] 2 SAM 23:39

Uriah to have such a beautiful wife. He had possibly even flirted with her on occasion, back when they were just a small band of fighting men. He must have known where she lived and where to stand on his roof if he wanted to catch a glimpse of her.

Though he had put Uriah out of his mind, Uriah had not forgotten him. And so this king who had once protected Saul from Uriah now found himself plotting to kill Uriah, who had only ever loved him. The wage of David's sin with Bathsheba was the death of his friend.

The Lord showed the prophet Nathan what David had done, and Nathan went to show it to David. Instead of jabbing a finger in the king's chest, Nathan told David a story.

Nathan said, "There was a man who had everything he could have ever wanted. Success, wealth, a beautiful wife, thousands of sheep in his flocks. He had a neighbor who had very little. The neighbor had no livestock except for one little ewe lamb, and he loved that lamb like a daughter. The rich man wanted to have a feast, but he didn't want to prepare a lamb from his own flock. So he took the little lamb his neighbor loved so much and slaughtered it instead."[4]

Anger rose up in David. "The man who did this deserves to die."[5]

Nathan took a breath and looked at the king. "You are that man."

The blood drained from David's face.

Nathan continued, "The Lord anointed you king over Israel. He delivered you out of Saul's hand. The hearts of the people are yours. And if all this wasn't enough, God would have given you more. So why, David, have you despised him? Why did you kill your friend and steal his wife?"[6]

---

[4] 2 SAM 12:1–4   [5] 2 SAM 12:5   [6] 2 SAM 12:7–9

The fog of David's scheming lifted, and he saw his sin for what it was. Repentance flowed from the deepest parts of his heart. He prayed, "Have mercy on me, O God. According to your unfailing love and great compassion, blot out my transgression and wash away all my iniquities. Cleanse me of my sin, because I know my sin is always before me. Against you, you only, have I sinned. I have done what is evil in your sight. You are right to judge me. Have mercy. Create in me a clean heart and put a right spirit in me. Please don't take your Holy Spirit from me as you did from Saul. Don't cast me away. Don't give up on me. Restore to me the joy of your salvation and uphold this broken man. Do it because you want to."[7]

David's heart was laid bare. He meant every word.

Nathan told the king, "The Lord has put away your sin. He will preserve your life. But because you struck down Uriah, you will live by the sword for the rest of your days."[8]

THE GREAT KING was a great sinner, but God would never leave him. As it had been since the days of Adam, God's promises didn't depend on anyone but himself to keep them.

David took Uriah's widow as his wife, and together they had more children. One of them was a boy they named Solomon. If David was Israel's warrior-king, Solomon would be their prince of peace.

The Lord gave Solomon great wisdom, establishing him as a righteous judge over God's people. For so long, God's people had wandered in and around the land the Lord swore to give to their forefathers, and under the umbrella of God's eternal promises, the people had lived a transient

[7] Ps 51:1–12   [8] 2 Sam 12:9–13

existence. But now, David and Solomon began to lay the cornerstones of a kingdom, establishing the house of the king and the temple of the Lord in Jerusalem.

Solomon, like his father, began his reign with a singular devotion to the Lord. But later, also like his father, he exchanged his fidelity to the God of his fathers for the pursuit of his own glory. And glory he found. The opulence he amassed was unlike anything the world had ever seen. Gold adorned the walls of his home and temple. Jerusalem sparkled like a diamond in the sand. Solomon took more than a thousand wives and concubines. And eventually Solomon, for all his wisdom, showed himself a fool by turning to worship other gods.[9]

The cycle of sin and rebellion against the Lord continued as it had since the patriarchs. Solomon's kingdom split in two—Israel to the north and Judah to the south. From that split came many other kings. Some honored God with their lives, but most did evil in the sight of the Lord. King Jeroboam reintroduced the worship of the Canaanite Baals, the same idols the judges died trying to eradicate.[10]

God's people were fracturing, and none of the kings from the line of David seemed equipped to save them. But the Lord didn't abandon them. He raised up prophets from among them to proclaim the judgment of the Lord. They called Israel to repent of their turning from God, and sometimes God's people responded.

One prophet, Elijah, squared off against the prophets of Baal to prove that the gods they worshiped were nothing but wood and stone. They built an altar to see which God would come and consume the sacrifices offered on it. The Lord put on a powerful display, consuming not only the

[9] 1 Ki 2:12–11:43   [10] 1 Ki 15:34

sacrifice, but the altar and the earth beneath it. The power of God terrified the people, and they fell to the ground, pleading, "The Lord, he is God! He is God!"[11]

But even that wasn't enough to turn their faithless hearts to repentance. The prophets warned the people that God would use the gentile nations around them as the executors of his discipline. Through the prophets, God warned them that while he was wholeheartedly bound to preserve his covenant promises to keep these people as his own, this didn't mean that he wouldn't discipline them in their idolatry and rebellion. He would raise up the nations around them to carry them out of this land they had only just begun to settle.

The Lord told Adam that a redeemer would come from Eve who would crush the head of the serpent. He told David that a king would come from his line who would reign forever. These two figures were one and the same. And he had to come, or all was lost.

Humanity's condition was beyond hope. The Israelites couldn't save themselves from their generational cycles of rejecting the Lord as their God. Could it be that Israel's golden years were behind her—that when David died, the kingdom of Israel died with him?

The people cried out, "We want a king, full of power, with a sword in his fist, full of wisdom and strength. Prophet, tell us—will there be another king like this?" More than anything, this is what the people wanted to know.

And the prophet Micah answered, "From you, O Bethlehem, small among Judah, a ruler will come, ancient and strong."[12]

---

[11] 1 Ki 18:1–40   [12] Mic 5:2

In the desert of their idolatry, the Lord told them, "As the rain and the snow come down from heaven and do not return there but water the earth, making it germinate and sprout, giving seed to the sower and bread to the eater, so shall be every word that proceeds from my mouth; it shall not return to me empty, but it shall accomplish that which I purpose, and shall succeed in the thing for which I sent it."[13]

His promises would not return empty. The serpent would be crushed. A king was coming, and of his government there would be no end.[14]

---

[13] Isa 55:10–11   [14] Isa 9:7

15

THE EDGE OF RUIN

ISAIAH 9:2, 6–7

N THE YEAR that King Uzziah died, around 740 BC, a prophet of Israel named Isaiah saw a vision of God sitting on a throne, lofty and exalted, with the train of his robe filling the temple. Angels stood above the Lord, each having six wings. With two wings they covered their faces. With two others they covered their feet. And with two they flew. They called out to one another saying, "Holy, holy, holy is the Lord of Hosts!"[1]

The foundations of the holy place shook as the angelic voices thundered. Smoke filled the temple. Isaiah was terrified. There, enveloped in the radiant glory of the holiness of the Almighty Maker of heaven and earth, Isaiah felt naked and translucent. His entire life was on open display: his unclean heart, his duplicitous motives, his foul mouth. All of it.

With his own eyes he saw the Holy One, and it wrecked him. He felt lost. "Woe to me," he cried, "I'm a man of

---

[1] Isa 6:1–3

unclean lips and I live among a people of unclean lips; and my eyes have just seen the King, the Lord of Hosts!"[2]

In the same moment, when he imagined his life would be snuffed out by the seraphs surrounding the Lord, one of them moved to the bowl of embers glowing in the altar of incense. The angel lifted the tongs, removed a solitary white-hot coal from the basin, and touched it to Isaiah's lips, searing them and saying, "Your guilt is taken away, Isaiah. Your sins are atoned for."[3]

Then the Lord himself spoke. "I have a message for my people. Whom will I send? Who will go for us?"

On hearing this, Isaiah erupted, "Me! I'm right here. Send me!"

The God of Isaiah's Scriptures did what he pleased for the sake of the glory of his own name. Lately it seemed that what pleased God the most was bending Israel over the fulcrum of his judgment and discipline.

It had been a hard couple of centuries. When God appeared to Abraham all those years before, he promised the patriarch that his descendants would become a great nation. God told him, "I will give to you and to your offspring after you the land of your sojourn, all of Canaan, for an everlasting possession, and I will be their God just as surely as I am yours."[4]

It was framed as an everlasting promise. But that covenant was cut so long ago, and over the span of years Israel had become a people walking in darkness.[5] "The Fear," as Abraham's grandson Jacob used to call God, gave them ten commands to keep, and all they had ever done was find ways to break them. Anyone who knew anything about

---

[2] Isa 6:5
[3] Isa 6:7
[4] Gen 17:8
[5] Isa 9:2

their history of infidelity to the Lord winced at certain memories of God's dealings with them.

In addition to this spiritually impoverished condition, Judah's Assyrian neighbors to the northeast, rising in strength, appeared to be surveying Judah's land as though it already belonged to *them*. Some of Isaiah's own countrymen swore that the bitter scent of Assyria blew in the wind as they slept, filling their lungs with the constricting inevitability of exile.

Everything now seemed unsettled and fragile. Abraham's descendants were in trouble, and they knew it. They sensed an impending need for rescue from Assyria. From themselves. Even from their God.

This would shape Isaiah's message.

The Lord told him, "Go and tell your people that they hear, but they don't understand. They see, but they don't perceive. Their hearts are dull, and I mean to keep them this way."[6]

"For how long, O Lord?" Isaiah asked.

The Holy One's reply was stark and chilling: "Until every house is empty. Until every city is destroyed. Until every last inhabitant of this land is carried far away from here. Everything is going to burn."[7]

This was almost impossible for Isaiah to comprehend. All his life, from the time he was a boy, he'd heard stories of heroes and the battles they won, of leaders and the odds they overcame, of villains and the heights from which they fell. He could picture them in his mind—David with his sling, Abraham with his knife raised above his son bound on the altar, Rachel capturing Jacob's heart, Solomon with his thousand wives. They were built into his understanding of who he was. Isaiah was one of them.

---

[6] ISA 6:9–10   [7] ISA 6:11–13

And so much of his people's story centered on how their very existence often hung by a thread. God had delivered them and had even given them victories over much greater armies. He had struck fear in the hearts of would-be attackers, leaving mighty nations trembling at the thought of tangling with Israel. For Isaiah, the *endurance* of Israel was one of the most compelling parts of her story. And for those who feared the Lord, they knew it was God alone who kept them alive. But God-fearing or not, Isaiah's people had grown accustomed to being rescued. It was how things went for them.

Now, though, the angel of the Lord was telling him that the wrath of God was coming to scorch the earth.[8] What little remained would be like a charred, desolate stump where a mighty oak used to stand. And that stump would be all that remained of God's people.[9]

The description called to mind the charred swaths cut through the timberland foothills of Judah during the dry season. The dry season was also the wildfire season, and once a part of the forest started to burn, there was nothing to do but get out of its path and wait. Nervous residents watched the smoke rise in the west, painting the evening sky a deep, blood red. And when the winds shifted eastward from the sea, the scent of cedar turned to cinder turned to smoke filled the air.

The distant fires smelled clean—as if the land were being scrubbed, purified. But people couldn't escape the reality that the ash settling around them was all that remained of mighty trees that never stood a chance. Such thoughts made even the mightiest of men feel vulnerable to ruin.

---

[8] Isa 9:19   [9] Isa 6:13

Would this be Israel's end? Ruin? Was that Isaiah's message?

The fires of exile would burn. But deep inside a charred stump would linger a holy remnant of life, buried and hidden, but very much alive.[10]

It wouldn't be the end, but neither would this be another story of rescue at the last minute. Exile was coming, and there was no getting around it. It would be taxing and terrible. And it would be cleansing. It would shape Israel's future in such a way that they would lose their grip on their identity as a people with a place, leaving them where their forefathers started—as a people with only a God, a name, and a promise.

As much as this news exhausted Isaiah, speaking it was only the beginning. What people did with his message would be where the real heavy-lifting happened. It could only bring about one of two reactions—the galvanizing of proud hearts against God,[11] or the calling of the contrite to repentance and the relief of an unburdened conscience.[12]

So tell them, Isaiah. Even as the sparks of Assyrian exile are fanning into flame, tell them God will send his Messiah. Tell them he hasn't forgotten his promise to Abraham, that he hasn't forgotten *them*. Tell those living under the blood red sky of the purifying fires that a new light is about to dawn.[13] Tell them that God's rescue is coming.

Isaiah did.

But from as far back as anyone could remember, there remained this irrefutable fact: God cannot be hurried. To be helped by God, it seemed, was to wait on him.

With Assyria poised to have their way, the people of Judah didn't think they had the luxury of time. They

---

[10] Isa 6:13
[11] Isa 28:13
[12] Isa 66:2
[13] Isa 9:2

needed to be rescued, redeemed, saved. But they knew that between the promise of a new dawn and the actual rising of that sun, hundreds of years might pass, leaving them with no alternative but to wait for God to send his Redeemer. What else could they do?

They could pray. They could pray with all their hearts.

Come. Messiah, come!

And they could fast so that their thoughts and consciences might be clear.

Come. Messiah, come!

They could study God's word so that their lives might better prepare a place for him, that they might usher in his advent. They could sing songs in the night over their children and over their beloved spouses.

Come. Messiah, come!

They could bid him come in the midst of their mourning, even with their cheeks still wet with the grief of death.

Come. Messiah, come!

Oh, that their Redeemer would come! But how, Isaiah wondered, could this be? How would his people even know the Messiah if they saw him?

"The Lord himself will give you a sign," the angel said. "Look, a virgin will conceive and bear a son, and she shall give him the name Immanuel."[14]

A virgin would have a son called "God with us." This is what he would be—the word of God made flesh and dwelling among his people.[15] And somehow, by his life, God's people would find life too. Somehow, in some way, this son of the virgin would form some kind of union with the heirs to God's covenant promise and he would become their salvation.[16]

---

[14] ISA 7:14   [15] JN 1:14   [16] JN 17

What glorious implications! God was at work in his world, responding perfectly in the fullness of time to every need, every wound, and every desire.

Someday, in a stable outside of Bethlehem, a child would be born. A son would be given. He would be wounded for his people's transgressions. He would be crushed for their iniquities. Upon him would be the chastisement that would bring them peace, and with his stripes we would be healed.

But first the Promised Land would succumb to the fires of Assyria's exile, leaving things so desolate that old men would stand at the edge of the ruins and struggle to recall her former glory.

16

I HAVE LOVED YOU

MALACHI 4

SSYRIA AND BABYLON swept through the Promised Land and carried the people of God into captivity. They consumed Israel's resources and destroyed their cities. They killed their livestock and burned their homes. They separated husbands from their wives and parents from their children.

They broke every heart in the land, and few would ever recover from it.

Eventually, the people were permitted to return home, which some did like refugees of war. Some, but not all. Some had gotten married in captivity and started new lives in a different land. Many died. Many others lost interest in being part of a nation whose God—the same God who promised to love them as his own with an everlasting love—allowed pagan nations like Assyria and Babylon to defile them.

How were they to understand the stories of the Lord calling his servant Abraham to be the father of the nation *they* had become? Yes, they had disobeyed his Law. Yes, they had idolatrous hearts. But what about God's promise to never leave them or forsake them? Where was he in all this?

They demanded that God give an account of himself. They thought of the Psalmist crying out in the dark night of his soul, "My God, my God! Why have you forsaken me? Why are you so far from saving me? Why are you so far from the words of my groaning? Oh my God, I cry by day but you don't answer me, and by night, but I find no rest."[1]

The Lord spoke to them in an oracle, a burden, through a prophet named Malachi.

"I have loved you," said the Lord.[2]

But the people didn't feel loved. How were they supposed to reconcile this statement with their experience? The two were at odds, leaving one of two possibilities—either God was lying, or they were so blind to the purposes of his work in their lives that they couldn't make sense of his love.

"How? How have you loved us?"[3]

As he did with Sarah when she laughed at his promise to give her a son, the Lord used this question as an opportunity to turn Israel's attention to him while he confronted their disbelief. Sarah's laughter was, at first, a laugh of turning away. Likewise, Israel's question was a statement thrown over their shoulders as the rhetorical flourish of their cynical despondency. But to the Lord, this was anything but a rhetorical question. If they were going to ask how he had loved them, he was going to answer.

Of all the ways the Lord could have answered them, he reminded them of two brothers: Jacob and Esau.[4] Even

---

[1] Ps 22:1–3, Mt 27:46   [2] Mal 1:2
[2] Mal 1:2   [4] Gen 25

while they were in Rebekah's womb, these boys struggled with each other. She asked God why, and he told her, "Two nations are in your womb, and two peoples from within you shall be divided; the one shall be stronger than the other, the older shall serve the younger."[5]

When the boys were born, Esau came first with Jacob following, grabbing at his brother's heel, and they haven't stopped fighting to this day. When Esau realized that Jacob had stolen his birthright, it was too late. He demanded that his father extend the blessing to him as well, but Isaac had nothing left to give, telling him, "Son, you'll never stop fighting. By your sword shall you live, and you shall serve your brother."[6]

Esau's descendants would become known as Edom. Jacob's descendants came to be known as Israel. And all that had been said of both brothers came to pass.

So how had God loved Israel? He called them to be his people. He set his blessing on the people of Jacob, not Esau.[7] In fact, God chose Jacob's line before he was born, before he had any chance of earning or disqualifying himself from God's promise.[8] God chose Jacob's line to be his people and vowed to be their God forever. And he still was.

But God wasn't finished with their question yet. The problem wasn't simply that they couldn't see God's love. It was that they couldn't see themselves in an honest light either. So the Lord showed them the condition they were really in. His love for them wasn't found simply in the fact that he had chosen them. In spite of everything they had become, he was *still* choosing them. This was the evidence of his love that they couldn't see. The God of their fathers

---

[5] GEN 25:23
[6] GEN 27:40

[7] MAL 1:2–5
[8] GEN 25:23, ROM 9:10–13

was as devoted to their redemption now as when he told Adam, Eve, and the deceiver that he would bring from the seed of the woman one who would crush the head of the serpent.[9]

But in the years since their return from exile, they had become jaded. They went through the motions of worshiping the Lord, but their hearts were far from him. They couldn't see the benefits of serving God, and in fact believed it was better not to.[10] Their worship was heartless because their hearts were faithless.

But there was still hope.

Through prophets like Malachi, the Lord painted for them a sweeping picture of what they had become. There was so much pain packed into their lives. So much frustration. So much sorrow. So much rebellion. The more the Lord spoke through his prophets to remind them of his law, the more they saw how completely they had broken it. The prophets took them to the edge of hopelessness, as though their entire history was little more than the story of a great promise unraveling, the story of its recipients pulling and pulling at the fringes of every good and sacred thing God had given until there was nothing left.

It was a hard message, but they had to hear it. To comprehend their reason for hope, they had to hear and understand the Lord's righteous indictment against them. Their guilt ran so deep. Their rebellion against the Lord had come to define them. As a nation *and* as individuals, they had failed. They had utterly failed, and God was judging them for it.

There would be no meeting God in the middle. Hope would flow only in one direction—from the King of heaven

[9] Gen 3:15   [10] Mal 3

116

and earth to the empty-handed heirs of his promise. His people were so poor in spirit that they couldn't even articulate what they needed saving from. So in an immeasurable gift of grace, their God would show them. They needed to be rescued, saved from their sin and sorrow. They needed to know God had not abandoned them to decay in their graves.[11]

So after his indictment against them, the prosecution rested. The Lord said, "For you who fear my name, the sun of righteousness shall rise with healing in its wings. You shall go out leaping like calves from the stall."[12]

Where there was despair, there would be hope. The sun of righteousness would rise. God's Rescuer would shine a light in every dark corner. Where the people now lived in danger, under constant threat of war or famine, God's refining work of salvation would bring security. Hope would break like the dawning of the sun.

Where there was brokenness, there would be healing. The sun of righteousness would rise with healing in its wings. As the sun brings life to whatever it shines upon, God's judgment would have a profound effect on his people, mending everything that was broken, making his people whole and alive in the warmth of a new day.

Where there was sadness, there would be joy. When the sun of righteousness rose on the people of God, they would go out leaping like calves. The solemn and sorrowful ones who only plodded through life would become like children who, wearing their joy like Joseph's robe, skip, run, dance, leap, and spin. In their gladness, they would no longer simply walk.

Where there was bondage, there would be freedom. Like calves leaping from a stall into an open field, they

---

[11] Ps 16:10   [12] MAL 4:2

would revel in their liberty. They had been cooped up, penned in, hunkered down. But the scent of spring hovered over everything as hope rose that there was life yet hidden in what the winter months destroyed. Though they had become acclimated to living in a hemmed-in kennel of a world, on that morning when the sun of righteousness rose with healing in its wings, a joy would overtake God's people, a sweetness would fill their lungs, and they would taste a new freedom.

How high would be the hope? How deep the healing? How long the joy? How wide the freedom? The Lord said, "Even to the extent that I will turn the hearts of fathers to their children and the hearts of children to their fathers."[13] For every father so consumed with his own prosperity that he never noticed the slow turning of his daughter's heart away from him, or for every mother so committed to her own glory that she never tended to her own son's need to know he was lovable, or for every child who fled like a prodigal from the discipline and shelter of home for the illusion of freedom in a land of strangers, there would be healing.

A page in history was about to turn. Though Israel's world was in the throes of upheaval, it was only a matter of time before the sun of righteousness would rise. These people needed rescue, but they weren't waiting for the stars to align or for the political climate to change. They were waiting for God. They were on *his* timetable. He was sending his Messiah—Immanuel, "God with us." It was a plan in motion. It would take some time—longer than anyone imagined. But deep inside the smoldering stump of Israel, a remnant of life was rising to push back the darkness

[13] MAL 4:6

and break through the crust of the desolation of the people of God to find the light of day.

Though they struggled to see it, God loved them. He loved them with an everlasting, unfailing love. Salvation was coming, and when all was said and done, "He will dwell with them and they will be his people and God himself will be with them as their God. He will wipe away every tear from their eyes, and death shall be no more, neither shall there be mourning, nor crying, nor pain anymore."[14]

"Behold," he says, "I am making all things new."[15]

---

[14] Rev 21:3–4   [15] Rev 21:5

17

HEROD THE GREAT, KING OF THE JEWS

MATTHEW 2:3

 T TU, BRUTE?"

While Julius Caesar lay dying, the members of his own senate stood over him, bloody daggers dripping in their hands.

A few years earlier, a civil war for the control of Rome had broken out between Julius Caesar and Pompey, who was married to Caesar's only child, Julia. The stability of Rome as a republic was failing, and factions favoring Caesar and others favoring Pompey developed. Julius Caesar prevailed in the civil war, and the defeated Pompey fled to Egypt. As Pompey drew near to the Egyptian port, what he thought was a welcoming party met his boat and killed him before he set foot on land.

Though Pompey's death undoubtedly led Caesar to breathe a little more easily, Caesar regarded his son-in-law's death as a tragedy and as a bad omen concerning the weakening of Rome—whose reach (which now included northern Africa, Judea, Idumea, and Syria) had already spread further than any one nation could expect to hold onto.

Caesar wasn't alone in his concern. Many of the ruling class feared for Rome's future. The present unrest awakened a sense of opportunism among the ambitious political, military, and civil would-be leaders, who began grassroots campaigns for power and control.

In 46 BC, the senate gave the heroic and popular Julius Caesar full authority to do whatever it took to bring stability back to Rome, granting to him the title of dictator. In 45 BC, the senate amended this title to be an appointment for life. Caesar became ruler of all things military and domestic—and took Rome from being a republic with a senate to being, for all practical purposes, an empire under a single ruler.

Julius Caesar grew in power and ambition. His hunger for control manifested itself in large building programs, which in turn required heavy taxation. This left his governors, such as Antipater the Idumean, procurator of Judah, in a quandary. Caesar had given Antipater his position as a reward for helping settle the unrest in Alexandria, but now the people under his governance were being taxed to the point of breaking, and they were looking to Antipater for relief.

Caesar's unchecked reach troubled the consciences of many of his governors, but whenever reports of their unrest reached his ears, he simply replaced them with new leaders whose loyalty wasn't yet in question (and some of those deposed leaders were never heard from again). But this was only a short-term fix. Before long, Caesar didn't know who was for him and who wanted him gone.

One of those who wanted him gone was a Roman senator named Cassius, and Cassius had a plan.

On March 15, 44 BC, when Caesar arrived for a meeting of the senate, a senator named Tillius Cimber approached him, begging the emperor to allow his politically exiled brother to return home without fear of retribution. Others crowded around the two men in support of Cimber. Caesar tried to wave him off, but Cimber grabbed Caesar by the shoulders, pleading with his emperor for mercy.

It was during this commotion that Cassius gave the signal and one of the senators rushed at Caesar with a knife. Caesar saw him coming, grabbed his arm, and deflected the blow, only to see many more daggers coming in hard and fast. The last thing Caesar saw as he lay dying was his own senate, which included even his most trusted friend Brutus, standing over him, his blood on their hands.

In that moment, though it wasn't formally pronounced, Caesar's power transferred to Cassius. Antipater of Idumea, like the rest of Caesar's staff, now had to decide where his loyalties lay—with the assassin of his emperor or with someone else. He chose Cassius.

Choosing loyalty to Cassius was a bit more complicated than simply declaring it. Cassius determined that, given the high cost of feigned loyalty (which Caesar's death so graphically illustrated), such an allegiance should be expensive enough to weed out the pretenders. The price he attached to peace was seven hundred talents—more than three times the annual income of many of the regions under Roman rule.

Seven hundred talents was a fortune few cities, let alone individuals, could afford, so Antipater decided that, for his part, he would collect the money through taxation. He divided his region into seven parts and assigned those parts to seven of his most reliable men. His son Herod was responsible for the region of Galilee.

Galilee was a tough region to rule. Over time it had become a haven for brigands—land-pirates who were choking out trade and chasing away any sense of safety in the region. For Herod to gather his portion of Cassius' wage for his father, he had to bring Galilee under his law, which meant putting down the lawless.

Herod got what he wanted. Though he never totally eliminated his opposition, he proved to be a shrewd tactician among the Galileans. Both his father and Cassius recognized in young Herod the skills and instincts of a leader.

One of the marks of Herod's leadership was his paranoia. The older he grew, the less he trusted anyone. He was mercilessly committed to sniffing out even the faintest hint of insurrection. And he usually found it—sometimes only in loose circumstantial evidence, but other times in assassination plots certainly already underway. Regardless, his retribution was swift and fatal. His reputation for ruthlessness in response to disloyalty was most evident in the growing list of wives and sons he had put to death for conspiring against him.

Two things Herod learned by watching his father's political career under the Roman system were that loyalties could change no matter how tight the bond and that daggers were easy to hide in the folds of a robe. He came by his paranoia honestly, and it most likely saved his life more than once.

Like his father before him, Herod was Idumean by blood. Idumea lay just south of Judea and consisted of Edomites who had been forced to convert to Judaism by the Hasmoneans—a group of militant Judeans determined to minimize Greek influence in the Promised Land. This meant Herod was part Jew, and he took his Jewish heritage seriously. He observed certain ceremonial laws and customs, including a kosher diet, which led one of his closest friends to observe that it was "better to be Herod's pig than to be his son."

Still, as fickle as Herod might have appeared to those watching him from a distance, there was a certain logic behind his volatility. Herod's family stood with their feet in two worlds—one in their inherited Judaism and the other in Roman politics. For Herod, both required a tight grip and a watchful eye.

Rome knew well how much political sensitivity was needed for maintaining peaceful control over a religious people—especially committed monotheists like the Jews. As far as Rome was concerned, Herod was everything they could ask for—politically sensitive and culturally aware.

Herod came from the right stock, and he had his priorities straight. His political ambitions outweighed his need to be accepted by the Jews. He didn't need to be accepted by the Jews if he could become their king. Then they would *have* to accept him.

Little by little, the senate of Rome gave Herod more power and responsibility, eventually naming him King of Judea, which by decree made him King of the Jews.

The world Herod inherited was recovering from the fallout of exile. The Land Between, this swath of promised land that joined Asia Minor to Palestine to Africa, had a history of being easy to take but nearly impossible to hold. The Assyrians who carried the Judeans off into exile lost their grip on the land to the Persians, who lost their grip to the Greeks, who lost their grip to the Egyptians, who lost their grip to the Syrians, who lost their grip to the Hasmoneans, who lost their grip to Rome.

Herod would not squander his opportunity. He knew what would be required of him, and he would meet those requirements. Herod's memory ran deep. He'd seen his father pledge his allegiance to one leader, only to give it to another when the seat of power shifted. He'd seen men from greater families than his rise and fall in the Roman Empire. He knew his own position was tenuous. He knew he was under constant evaluation, and he needed to maintain every appearance of control.

Herod had the best resources Rome had to offer at his disposal—soldiers, money, the force of law. He could do almost anything he pleased to compel the people under his charge to cooperate with his governance. But he did not have enough power to empty a people of their faith, and the people he ruled were a people of faith.

Herod knew their memories ran deep too. They were a people rich in heritage and identity. They were a proud, strong nation. They were survivors—survivors of Egyptian slavery, of wilderness wanderings, of wicked kings, and now of exile. They held certain days and certain places as holy. They professed faith in one God because they only believed in One God.

And they also believed in a Messiah—a coming king. As broken and emptied out as they had become since the golden years of King David, they still held to the idea that they would once again become a mighty nation.

When the Hebrew people returned from exile, they began to sift through the ruins of their once great nation, slowly stacking the stones that remained, one on top of another. They weren't just rebuilding a war-ravaged landscape, they were trying to rebuild their broken theology as well.

God had promised to take the Hebrew people as his own and to keep them forever. So what was the exile? Had God abandoned them? Had he forsaken his promise? Was there any life left in the roots of Judah? They could rebuild the buildings, but everyone knew they couldn't reconstruct the past.

Still, there remained deep roots of faith—hope in a not-quite-forgotten promise. Yes, Rome held the power for now, but as far as the children of Abraham were concerned, this too would pass. A remnant of faith remained in them, and Herod knew it. For as long as he ruled over them, he would never forget it.

18

THE SILENCE OF
THE PRIEST

LUKE 1:1–25, 57–80

HERE WERE MEN among the twelve tribes of Israel who must have possessed a mysterious aura in the imaginations of children— men who always smelled like smoke and iron and were often spattered with blood.

When one of these men passed by on the street, the children stared as their parents explained that that man's work was bloody because it was holy. That man was a priest, and the scent of the blood he wore was the residue of the sacrifices he offered on the behalf of the people.

That river of blood flowed as far back as any of them could recall, all the way back to their slave days in Egypt when their ancestors sacrificed a lamb and smeared its blood over the doorposts of their homes.

God's people grew up in a culture of sacrifice and spoke the language of sacrifice. Without the shedding of blood there was no forgiveness of sins, they said. So the priesthood carried over from one generation to the next, along with their bloody work, all the way down to the time of an old cleric named Zechariah.

Zechariah and his wife Elizabeth were both descendants of Moses' brother Aaron, the first priest of Israel. There was never much of a question what Zechariah would do when he came of age. He would become a priest, in the manner of the generations before him.

As a priest, Zechariah was scheduled to serve in the temple in Jerusalem for two weeks out of the year. On one particular occasion, it was his responsibility to go into the temple to burn incense to the Lord. This was an honor that came once in a lifetime. But when Zechariah entered the temple, at the right side of the altar of incense stood an angel of the Lord named Gabriel.

Terror filled Zechariah, as it filled anyone who had ever seen an angel from heaven. In Gabriel, Zechariah saw his own fragility. With a word, surely the angel could return this priest to the dust from which he had come. Was this the reason for his visit? Had Zechariah taken his unworthiness to enter the holy presence of God for granted?

"Don't be afraid," Gabriel said. It was a small comfort, but Zechariah had no time to think as the angel continued, "The cry of your heart has been heard."

Which cry? His priestly prayers for God to deliver his people? His yearning for a sacrifice that would sufficiently atone for the sins of his countrymen? That cry?

Or was it the sorrow he shared so intimately with the wife of his youth concerning their inability to have children? It hurt his heart just to think of it. He recalled the two of them, young, in love, and ready to become a family. But something was wrong, something with one or the other or both. Who could say? All he knew was that, try as they might, God had shut Elizabeth's womb. And now in their old age, bearing a child would require a miracle.

"Your wife Elizabeth will bear you a son. You're to give him the name John."

The aging priest's heart leapt. He wanted to believe, but why would the angel appear in the temple to tell him *this*? And why now?

Zechariah grew up with the stories of Abraham and Sarah and Isaac and Rebekah. He knew God could and sometimes did open barren wombs, giving him a flicker of hope that maybe his story would be like these. Maybe he too was being invited into this wonderful tale of God's loving-kindness. But what if he allowed himself to hope only to be disappointed?[1]

"Listen, priest. This son of yours will turn many of the children of Israel to the Lord their God, and he will go before him in the spirit and power of Elijah, to make ready for the Lord a people prepared."[2]

It wasn't just his cry for a son that the Lord had answered. God was responding to the cry of his people for deliverance. He meant to use this son to prepare the way for the coming of his Redeemer.

But Zechariah wanted proof. "We're so old. How can I know this will happen?"

Gabriel replied, "I am Gabriel, who stands in the presence of God." If the appearance of an angel of the Lord wasn't enough, another sign could be arranged. Zechariah would be plunged deep into a world of silence, unable to speak, where he would remain until the birth of this promised child. No whispering to the baby in Elizabeth's growing belly. No telling his neighbors about this son he

---

[1] Rom 5:1–5   [2] Lk 1:17

had been waiting for his entire life. Only silence—nine months of it.

It was bittersweet, but this silence was a gift. Zechariah was given time to think, time to remember the words and the physical frame of the Guardian of Heaven whose apparition, for some reason, was easier to accept than the words that he spoke.

To worship God is to dwell on who he is, to consider his handiwork.[3] Often worship requires stillness. Stillness allows a mind to hold complicated thoughts without losing them. Silence was a gift God gave to Zechariah, and the old man put it to work.

He had enough time to rebuke himself for his doubt and plenty left over to contemplate what God was doing. He thought of his own need for salvation and God's promise of it. He thought of the man he had become and of the priesthood and of God's displeasure with his people's rebellion against him.

He thought of the ocean of blood his own hands had spilled, and how if he were to spill all the blood of all the priests of every generation, it still wouldn't come close to being enough to atone for the sins of Israel or, for that matter, the sins of Zechariah.

He thought of Scripture and of history. He thought of the angel's words and his own role in God's redemption.

And he thought of his son. Would his boy really turn the hearts of many to the Lord his God?

From Elizabeth's first bout with nausea to that day nine months later when they, along with their astonished kinsfolk, laid their tired eyes on this brand new baby boy, Zechariah held his peace. God used this silence to persuade

---

[3] Job 37:14

the old minister that God *was* sending his salvation to his people, and that this miracle baby was brought into the world to herald the Messiah's coming.

In those days, a son was his father's honor, and tradition dictated that the firstborn son take his father's name. When the boy turned eight days old, they would circumcise him and announce that name—the name he would go by all his days as a member of the covenant family of God.

When the son of Zechariah and Elizabeth was circumcised on the eighth day, his aunts, uncles, cousins, nieces, and nephews waited for his parents to formally introduce little "Zechariah."

Elizabeth gave her mute husband a penetrating look. His eyes told her what she needed to say on his behalf. "We are going to call him John."

John? Why? There was no one in their family who went by that name.

For a moment it must have seemed like it was Elizabeth against the world. Her relatives looked to Zechariah, as if his wife might have somehow been taking advantage of his silence. Was he going to allow this?

He stepped between his wife and her detractors. Pinching his forefinger to his thumb, he motioned for something to write on. The note he scribbled was short and resolute. On the tablet were four words in Zechariah's own hand: "His name is John."

And that was that. This baby was John.

"John?" The kinfolk tried it out like a question, speaking the name to the child as if to gauge his response. As they cooed and sang the name over him, a familiar voice in the corner of the room rose from a murmur to a crescendo.

"His name is John!"

Zechariah wept as words flowed from his lips in a symphony of awe and joy. Within minutes, everything that had been on his heart those past nine months came flowing out. To their amazement, he had little to say about his encounter with the angel or even his doubts about Elizabeth's ability to conceive.

Instead, Zechariah wanted to talk about the salvation of the Lord. All God's promises to Abraham and David were going to be fulfilled in the coming of God's Messiah. History was converging on this moment, and Zechariah understood that he and Elizabeth had been given this son because the world was being given a Savior.

Their son was born to prepare the way for the Messiah. And his name was John.

Then Zechariah got down nose to nose with his little boy: "You, my son, will proclaim the salvation of the people of God and the forgiveness of their sins. You exist to proclaim his mercy, just as your very life is God's mercy to us. A new light is dawning, and this message is the reason God gave you to us."

These were the words of a man who had had time to think.

Zechariah understood that though his life's work as a priest was insufficient and thus unending, if God were to preside as the priest over his people, and if he were to select the atoning sacrifice his people needed, that sacrifice would be sufficient. It would be perfect. And the river of blood would cease to flow from the heart of the Holy Place where God's presence dwelt.

The old priest would be among the last of his kind.

When the Lord loosed Zechariah's tongue, everyone present felt the weight of John's divine purpose. What would this child become? This question gave rise to so many others. "If the Messiah is coming and his people are called to bear witness to him, what then will *our* lives be? What will our sons' lives be? What will our daughters' lives be?"

Zechariah's benediction over John gave the answer.

They would be God's.

19

THE ORDINARY OVERSHADOWED

LUKE 1:26–38

LIZABETH HAD A cousin, a girl named Mary, who was engaged to a young man named Joseph. They lived in an out-of-the-way town called Nazareth. Joseph was descended from the great King David, though for his part he was a common laborer, a carpenter.

They were simple, honest people, dreaming and working toward a life they could live out together as husband and wife and, God willing, as a family. They probably expected to be ordinary in every way and perfectly happy for it.

But all this was interrupted in a moment when the angel of the Lord—the same one who visited Zechariah six months earlier—appeared to Mary and told her something that would alter the course of her and her husband's lives—and for that matter, the world itself.

The angel said to Mary, "Greetings, you who are highly favored! The Lord is with you."

Though the angel's words were friendly, Mary feared for her life. What could this messenger of the great I Am possibly have to say to her?

Mary belonged to a people familiar with the word of God. She grew up under its teachings. Since she was a little girl, laced throughout her lessons about Abraham, Isaac, Jacob, Joseph, Moses, and David was the prophetic foretelling of God's promised Messiah.

Young and old tried to imagine what his advent would lead to. Would the Lord's salvation come in a radiant swell of angelic fury? Would deliverance take the form of a mighty army rolling over Rome with some mythic warrior-king leading the charge? Down through the generations, the people tried to imagine it.

When the angel Gabriel stood before Mary, the hypothetical gave way to the real. The ordinary stories all at once glistened under the extraordinary light of this celestial storyteller.

As she listened, there rose inside her a sense that the glory of his tale was nothing new, but rather was older than time. She only needed uncommon light to see it. She had, Gabriel told her, found favor with God. She shouldn't fear this visit or the message he brought.

It must have been strange to stand before this seraph dressed in light, strong and otherworldly, and hear him tell her not to be afraid. Perhaps it was even stranger for Mary to discover that God had formed an overall impression of her. She was *known* by God, and he favored her. He liked what he saw?

The angel then came to the reason for his visit. He told Mary she would conceive a son, who would rescue his people from their sins. God had already chosen his name—Jesus, which meant "salvation."

But the message of the angel did not come without consequence for Mary and Joseph. It would lead these two young people to live as fugitives for a time, fleeing from the paranoia of a ruthless and powerful Roman ruler. And on top of all that, as her belly expanded, Mary and Joseph would have to endure the suspicious looks of friends and relatives who couldn't help questioning her purity and his character. Eventually, as an old cleric named Simeon would later predict, the anguish accompanying the consequences of this angel's news would be like a sword that would pierce through Mary's very soul.[1]

All this was coming, and so much more.

The angel continued with his message. Mary's boy would grow to reign over the people of God as their savior and king. God, who had promised David so many years before that his royal line would see no end, would keep that ancient covenant by bringing an heir to Israel's throne through this young woman.

"But how can this be, since I'm still a virgin?" she asked. For her to bear this son, she must conceive. And how can a virgin conceive?

The angel explained that all the laws of nature are amendable by the One who wrote them. Mary lived in the world that was made, and the Maker of this world was the sole author of what could and would happen here. The Holy Spirit would overshadow her, and when he pulled that shadow back, this virgin would become a mother to a son. *How* this would happen was less important than the fact that it *would*. And God would be the one to do it.

Knowing his words required a shift in her understanding of how the world worked, the angel gave Mary

---

[1] Lk 2:35

a sign to help her believe. If Mary would only go visit her elderly cousin Elizabeth who had been barren her entire life, she would find a woman only months away from having a miracle baby of her own. Elizabeth was now six months pregnant. This, the angel told Mary, was a sign that she might understand that nothing was impossible with God.

Now it was Mary's turn to speak. Wrapped in the vertigo of this inter-terrestrial conversation, she answered simply, "May it be done to me as you have said."

What else could she say?

The angel's message was as much about the character of the God who favored Mary as it was about what he meant to do for his people through her.

AFTER THE ANGEL'S visit, Mary set out for her cousin's house in the hill country of Judah. Elizabeth was resting inside when she heard someone call from the doorway. The voice was familiar, but it wasn't the familiarity that caught her interest. What grabbed her attention was how the little boy in her womb leapt at the sound of the greeting—as if he too knew her voice.

When she saw Mary, Elizabeth somehow understood that she and her cousin had something more than pregnancy in common. God was at work in the world, and for reasons higher than their understanding, the babies growing in their bellies would be at the center of it.

She pulled Mary close, embraced her, and said, "Blessed are you among women, and blessed is the fruit of your womb. Why am I so blessed that the mother of my Lord should come to me? Mary, when I heard your voice, the baby in my womb leaped for joy."[2]

---

[2] Lk 1:42

To hear Elizabeth frame it like that—that Mary was the mother of her Lord—solidified in Mary's heart that all of this was really happening, but she couldn't do anything to prepare for it. Neither could she help it along. Everything the angel told her was something that had to be done *for* her—something only God could do.

As Mary turned over the story unfolding before her—the story with roots as deep and ancient as the world itself, a song of praise welled up inside her.[3]

> *My soul magnifies the Lord,*
> *and my spirit rejoices in God my Savior,*
> *for he has looked on the humble estate of his servant.*
> *Behold, from now on all generations will call me blessed;*
> *for he who is mighty has done great things for me,*
> *and holy is his name.*
>
> *And his mercy is for those who fear him*
> *from generation to generation.*
> *He has shown strength with his arm;*
> *he has scattered the proud in the thoughts of their hearts;*
> *he has brought down the mighty from their thrones*
> *and exalted those of humble estate;*
> *he has filled the hungry with good things,*
> *and the rich he has sent empty away.*
>
> *He has helped his servant Israel,*
> *in remembrance of his mercy,*
> *as he spoke to our fathers,*
> *to Abraham and to his offspring forever.*[4]

This was the song her heart sang, but what would Joseph think?

---

[3] Lk 2:19   [4] Lk 1:46–55, ESV

20

WHEN JOSEPH WOKE FROM HIS DREAM

MATTHEW 1:18–25

OSEPH COULDN'T RECALL the first time he held a chisel and hammer, but as soon as he was able to begin his apprenticeship, his father put in his hands the tools of their family's industry. From as far back as he could remember, his palms bore the calluses of a laborer and his hair the sawdust of a craftsman.

He came from a line of builders and technicians who cultivated the skills of making useful things out of materials drawn from the dust of the earth. They were proud people.

Joseph learned to see ordinary objects through an artist's eye. To him, a table was more than a table. It told the story of a long line of problems and the decisions made to solve them—of beauty and structural integrity working together in balance, strong enough to hold a feast and lovely enough to draw people to it. And a table tells the truth about its craftsman. It shows the range of his skill, the artistry of his imagination, and the truth of his touch. It cannot lie.

No carpenter considered his work to be novel. Work wasn't so much about inventing new methods as it was mastering old ones. There was dignity in mastering a trade passed down through the generations. But to do this, a man had to yield himself to a life of discipline.

Joseph learned early that his was a world of structure and order. There were processes he had to follow if he wanted the things he made to hold together. Sloppy work and skipped steps didn't just weaken his handiwork, it weakened his name.

This was, of course, a principle that crossed over into all other areas of his life. In every matter of community, work, and faith, men were subject to process, order, and structure. So when his betrothed was suddenly expecting a baby, Joseph wasn't sure what to do. Things were out of order. He loved her, but she had betrayed his trust.

Joseph was a decent man. He didn't want to shame her, though he could have and no one would have blamed him. But he didn't want to lose her either. What could he do? His bride-to-be was pregnant, and he wasn't the father. His world was spinning. This burden weighed heavily on his heart, flooding his thoughts and his dreams.

Joseph wasn't a complicated man. He was honest and hard-working—noble in ancestry and character. He dreamed of one day having a son of his own to whom he would teach the family trade. He dreamed of married life. He dreamed of a home of his own. He dreamed of the respect of his community.

But Mary's condition threatened all of that, waking the young man from his dreams to a harsh reality. He knew the moment approached when he would have to act. And when he considered his options, his heart ached.

One night as he tossed and turned, an angel of the Lord appeared to him in a dream. He had come to set something straight. This baby was *not* forming in Mary's belly because of anything she had done. This was something *God* had done—something God was doing, part of the order and structure of his divine purpose.

"She will bear a son, conceived of the Holy Spirit, and you, Joseph, will name him Jesus, because he will save his people from their sins."[1] There was a purpose in this for both Joseph and Mary—she would bear the child, he would name him, and the child would save them from their sins.

Was this what the prophet Isaiah meant when he foretold that a virgin would conceive and have a son who would be called Immanuel—God with us?[2] This virgin Isaiah spoke of, could this really be *his* Mary?

The prophet Isaiah had a tough job at a rough time in Israel's history, and his ministry had become a sober part of every Israelite's story ever since. God had called Isaiah to relay the news of the Lord's coming judgment of his people. God had dispatched Assyria to carry his own people out of their homes and away into foreign lands. Babylon would bring a second wave of discipline.

But through Isaiah's words flowed a magnificent description of God's plan to save and redeem this same people who had rebelled against him over and over again. These were the stories Joseph and Mary grew up on, stories of colossal failure and of magnificent hope, stories of judgment and of salvation.

But what would God's salvation look like? As a boy, Joseph must have listened to the men around his home speculate. Would the people's ideas of that redemption bear

---

[1] Mt 1:21   [2] Isa 7:14

any resemblance to the rescue God actually meant to give? After all, it was an utterly novel thought that this girl who caused his heart to flutter would carry in her womb the Son of God, the promised and coming Savior who could carry the governments of the world on his still-forming shoulders.

Joseph might have recalled God's great qualifier in Isaiah's book: "As the heavens are higher than the earth, so are my ways higher than your ways and my thoughts higher than your thoughts."[3] As the heavens are higher than the earth? How much higher is that?

Salvation was such a paradox. The Israelites had ideas of what they thought they needed. For as long as Joseph could remember, God's people had looked to the east for their king to arrive in majesty, convinced they would know him when they saw him.

So why, then, was God quietly sending his angel to a poor teenage girl and her fiancé in the no-account town of Nazareth?

Joseph rehearsed what he could remember from Isaiah, contrasting it with the common ideas he grew up hearing. God's people expected the Messiah to be known by all upon his arrival. Would God really announce his coming under the cover of darkness? God's people anticipated a Messiah of unparalleled strength. Would they really be given a fragile, tiny baby?[4] Wouldn't he inspire the masses? Wouldn't the people instinctively know to follow him? Or, as Isaiah said, would the true Messiah be countless times *rejected*?[5]

The people of Israel longed for their suffering and oppression to end with the Savior's coming. Would he

---

[3] ISA 55:9   [4] ISA 7:14   [5] ISA 53:3

really come to suffer and live a life of affliction himself? Would he really take upon himself the wounds of God's children and die under their weight?[6]

As Joseph weighed the implications, he thought of the names the angel had used for this baby—Jesus, meaning "God will save," and Immanuel, meaning "God with us." Together, these names came together to describe who this baby would be and what he would accomplish—the Savior, God with us.

God was bringing his ancient plan to fruition, a plan forged in the void of the vast expanse that existed before the world was made, and Mary was somehow part of it. So was Joseph. They were part of it because the baby in Mary's womb was at the center of it, as he had somehow been since before time. Her son would be the consolation of her people, Israel. He would be their king, and of his kingdom there would be no end.[7]

The angel said, "Son of David, do not fear to take Mary as your wife, for that which is conceived in her is from the Holy Spirit. She will bear a son, and you will call him Jesus because he will save his people from their sins."[8]

Joseph woke from his dream and for the first time in a while felt like a man who knew what he was supposed to do. He was supposed to believe. To believe God, and to believe Mary. He was supposed to love her, take care of her, and keep her as safe and secure as he could.

So he married that girl, and together they set out for his hometown to register as a family. And Joseph told Mary, "When he comes, his name will be Jesus," because the angel said he will save his people from their sins.[9]

---

[6] Isa 53:5
[7] Isa 9:7
[8] Mt 1:20–21
[9] Mt 1:24–25

21

It Was Not a Silent Night

Luke 2:1–7

AZARETH TO BETHLEHEM was a long journey. Weeks had passed, and they'd exhausted nearly every topic of conversation they could think of, including the details of the strange things they had seen and heard over the past year. They spoke of angels, of dreams, of their hopes for their people, and of their love and fear of God.

The people of the cities and camps where they lodged along the way didn't know much about Joseph and Mary. They could see that he was earnest and driven and that she was pregnant and about to burst.

But this couple carried a holy secret, whispered into their ears by the lips of an angel and conceived in the warmth of her womb by the overshadowing Spirit of God. It played like a distant symphony, building in its movements and phrases to a coming crescendo that would shake the foundations of the world. But for now it remained a quiet, distant sound pulsing in the hearts of the man and his bride.

To their amusement—and to her discomfort—the baby often turned and kicked. They hadn't planned to spend the final weeks of her pregnancy on the road, but this miracle didn't suspend life as they knew it. The extraordinary work of God and the ordinary business of living under Roman occupation ran in tandem. So when the order to register for the Roman census coincided with the final weeks of Mary's pregnancy, it meant a trip to Bethlehem. They had to go.

FOR ALL OF Rome's obvious strength of force, evidenced by the growing list of occupied nations under her rule, it was not beyond her to use a softer touch to reach her objectives. The decree for the census had come down from Caesar Augustus himself, but it was up to Quirinius, the governor of Syria, to carry it out. The question before Quirinius was this: How do you direct Israel, a nation of committed monotheists, to cooperate with Caesar's edict that they become registered tax-payers to Rome, a nation of committed polytheists? A central characteristic of a theology that embraces only one true God is the passionate rejection of all others.

Militarily, Rome held all the cards. Israel held no power except what their passion for the one true God stirred in their hearts. But Quirinius knew Caesar's census would strike close to the heart of these people—obligating them to pay taxes that would fund temples and the perpetuation of the story that Caesar was himself a god. Quirinius knew this could become not just a costly drain on his own personnel and resources but an embarrassing reflection on what could be interpreted as his ineptitude as a leader.

So did the implementation of this census call for brute force or delicate discretion? This was the governor's problem. Maybe there was some sort of diplomatic process already in place. Maybe he could satisfy Caesar's decree by marrying it to a custom already built into the Jewish way of life—one that might help them feel that the census was as much for their records as it was Rome's.

Quirinius knew that Israel's great King David took a similar census generations before according to the various clans of Israel.[1] This was the solution. The census would follow King David's model. The people would register according to tribal heritage.

ALTHOUGH JOSEPH LIVED in Nazareth in the region of Galilee, he was descended from the great king himself, and thus he was Judean. So when the edict came down, he and Mary set off for Bethlehem, the City of David.

The closer they got, the more travelers clogged the streets. In the long line of dispersed Judeans all on the same mission, it seemed Joseph and Mary were among those bringing up the rear.

Joseph asked around but couldn't find a place to stay, not even at the inn. Every room was full, except for a stable. It wasn't much, but it was dry, warm, and at least had the potential to offer Mary a comfortable place to sleep. Besides, they were tired. The stable would be fine.

HER LIPS PURSED as she sucked in short breaths of air. Her belly went tight as a drum. She looked worried, unsure—as if her mind and her body had all at once become strangers to one another. And then as quickly as it rose, the pain subsided. Joseph was at her side, willing and eager to do whatever he could, though there didn't seem to be much for him to do.

---

[1] 2 SAM 24

With the shafts of moonlight on her face, she looked beautiful—young but not quite like the girl she was when they first met. In a certain light, that girl was still there, but her features had deepened. And so had his vision.

Between the angels, the pregnancy, the wedding, and the census, the theme of the past year had been about listening to the story of who they were. They weren't children anymore, but they didn't quite feel like grown-ups either. They were somewhere between who they used to be and who they were becoming, and there was no place in the world Joseph wanted to be more than right there at Mary's side.

Minutes later the pain stabbed at her again, only this time it was worse. Then it happened again. And again.

Joseph busied himself, though he wasn't sure what he was supposed to be doing. *Make room*, he thought. *Carve out some space for her to have this baby.* There was no one around to coach them, no one to tell them everything would be all right.

He held her and he prayed.

They thought of the angels who visited their dreams. They thought of Adam and Eve taking the forbidden fruit and how one of the consequences of that act of rebellion was shooting through Mary from head to toe, every three minutes now.

It was not a silent night. She strained and groaned and fought for every breath. She pushed as sweat beaded on her forehead. Joseph wiped her brow and told her a hundred times that he loved her, he loved her, he loved her.

Swept up in waves of pain and contractions, Mary continued to push and breathe and strain while time passed. Eventually, as if cresting a ridge, her labor gave way to delivery, and her groaning gave way to the sound of the cries and the coos of little lungs drawing in the breath of earth for the first time.

Joseph laid the baby on Mary's chest, and to the wonder of the helpless man and the relief of the weary woman, they beheld him who, though he was the Son of God, was every bit a fragile, tiny baby.

The little stranger was nothing like Mary imagined—not because he looked different from other babies, but because the face of a newborn has little room for distinctive features. It would be a while before this child's wide eyes would stare into hers or his baby fat would fill in the wrinkles around his neck and thighs.

But one thing was certain. He was beautiful.

She loved everything about him—his tiny nose, his wisps of dark hair, his perfect little fingers and toes. The sound of his first cry was the loveliest tune she had ever heard. It was as if this baby had gone from being her burden to being her physician, healing the toll her pregnancy had taken on her body simply by lying across her breast, absorbing her warmth.

Together, Mary and her husband cleaned him and wrapped his little arms and legs in strips of cloth to keep him warm. When they laid him in a manger and finally exhaled, they gave him the name Jesus. And both remembered why.

The incarnation of the Savior of the world could have come to pass in any number of ways. But God, in his infinite wisdom, chose this couple for this night in this shelter. This boy, the angel had told them, would be the heir to David's throne. He would be their wonderful counselor, their mighty God, their everlasting Father, their Prince of Peace. The government would be upon his shoulders.[2]

---

[2] Isa 9:2–7

But there was nothing particularly complex or regal about this moment in the stable outside Bethlehem. There were no heralds in the streets announcing the birth of a king. By all appearances, it was a humble, simple affair, seemingly unconnected to everything else going on in David's town that night.

But it wasn't inconsequential. It was the most significant moment in the history of the world. There on the edge of Bethlehem, a child was born. A son was given. And the zeal of the Lord Almighty accomplished this.[3]

---

[3] Isa 9:7

22

WHERE THE LAMBS ARE KEPT

LUKE 2:8–15

HE POOR YOU will always have with you."[1] Down through the ages and around the globe, the desperate and poor have huddled and scraped and stretched out their tired hands, hoping for the kindness of strangers to lift them up, even if just a little.

And down through those same ages, around that same globe, people have silently wondered how the poor among them came to such desolation. Their speculations often ventured close enough to the truth to become educated guesses—widening even more the chasm between the haves and the have-nots.

But no one has a simple story. The tale of any man in the grip of poverty is one of great defeat, regret, and heartache. But it isn't always obvious to the casual observer. Sometimes the poverty is hidden away in the heart behind tight lips and hard eyes.

---

[1] MT 26:11

For some it's a hand dealt late in life. Others are born into it, and it's all they know. But either way, poverty is a relative notion: it's when one person lacks what the rest seem to have. So the poor of a community often become a community of their own—a place where help is given, where dreams are welcomed without ridicule, where what resources they do have are respected as useful. Down through the ages and around the globe, groups of people joined together by their poverty of reputation have formed communities within their communities in order to work and live out the days appointed for them by their Maker.

Such were the shepherds of Bethlehem.

The shepherd's life was ironic. Their job was to care for the animals that would be sacrificed to atone for the sins of the people. Yet because of their handling of these dirty creatures, they themselves were unclean and thus prevented from keeping the ceremonial law. And because they were ceremonially unclean, they were often regarded as untrustworthy, irreligious, and poor in reputation.

Nevertheless, it was also expected that one who did his job well, a *good* shepherd, would be willing to lay down his life for his sheep.[2] A good shepherd was someone who cared deeply for the lambs under his watch, many of which were appointed to die on the altar of the Lord for the sins of the very people who looked down on the shepherds.

The shepherds' lives were, in effect, sacrifices.

On one particular night, in the pastureland skirting Bethlehem's northeast side, some shepherds sat like sentinels at their posts, keeping watch over their flocks, unaware of the angel regarding them from the skies overhead.

---

[2] Jn 10:11

What would an angel think of their strange vocation? It was God's idea that in this world sheep would depend on shepherds to watch over them. The Maker could have made them differently—and yet there sat the musty men with their staffs and their rods, cooperating with the order of creation, lest the beasts under their care perish. Though their solitary work afforded them many silent nights except for the words they chose to speak or sing over their flocks, this night would be different.

A sudden, glorious light shone in the darkness as the angel of the Lord appeared among them. The shepherds were terrified. Of course they were. So wide was the gap between God and man that whatever information an angelic messenger was dispatched to deliver seemed more likely to be bad news than good. They were afraid because they knew they had *reason* to be afraid.

But the angel said, "Don't be afraid. Listen, I bring you good news of great joy that will be for all the people!"

The angel's words painted a picture of the glorious presence of the promised Redeemer. He used names to describe the coming Messiah to these shepherds—names that spoke to the Messiah's purpose. He called him the Savior, meaning that he would atone for the sins of the people. He called him Christ, distinguishing him as their deliverer. He called him the Lord, identifying him as divine.[3]

The shepherds might have wondered why the angel chose to reveal this to them. This sort of news seemed to belong to people of influence or nobility. It was hardly the kind of report they ever imagined would be exclusively for men of their vocation, let alone reputation. But then the angel used one more expression that brought overwhelming

[3] Lk 2:11

clarity to this moment. He told them that Christ the Lord had been born "unto *you*."[4] The divine Savior and Messiah had been born unto *them*!

Though they lived most of their lives on the outside looking in, they would not be outsiders to this gift. They were the recipients of it.

This was big news. The shepherds sensed it, but the angels in heaven *knew* it, and their behavior offered a glimpse into the cosmic weight of this announcement. Initially, it was just one glorious but solitary angel who appeared to these men in Bethlehem's fields. But as soon as he announced Jesus' birth, "suddenly there was with the angel a multitude of the heavenly host praising God."[5]

It was as if there were millions of angels hiding just behind some celestial door, and once they heard, "Unto you is born this day a Savior, who is Christ the Lord!" they were unable to contain their joy any longer and all rushed in, praising God, singing, "Glory to God in the highest, and on earth peace among those with whom he is pleased."

For the poor, helplessly earthbound shepherds, this was a lot to take in. What had they just heard? What did it mean? How should they respond? Wisdom suggested that if the angelic hosts of heaven offered unfettered joy in response to this message, their reaction was appropriate. Though none of those shepherds had ever before had an angel of the Lord tell them of the coming of the Savior of the world, the spontaneous eruption of angelic praise became the lens through which they would see this moment: God was at work. This much was plain. But why had the glory of all glories appeared to the lowest of the lows? Why had the angel chosen to reveal this message to mere shepherds, unclean as they were?

---

[4] Lk 2:11   [5] Lk 2:13

Because poverty is relative. Could it be that from the perspective of heaven, the poor shepherds outside Bethlehem were no more or less poor than the rest of the world sleeping under its watch? Could it be that the poor of the earth were in fact *all* the people of the earth—poor in spirit, mourning and meek, hungry and thirsty for righteousness?[6] Could it be that the Savior's coming was for them as much as it was for anyone, and for anyone as much as it was for them?

The angels gave the shepherds a sign that left them speechless. Their Messiah and Savior could be found where the young lambs were kept. He would be the one not covered in wool, but wrapped in a swaddling cloth.

Where the lambs are kept? This they needed to see.

When they found Jesus in the manger as the angel said, the very location of his birth was drenched in significance. The Savior had been born into their unclean world in the same manner as a lamb. The symbolism was not lost on them.

When the shepherds saw Jesus there, they not only saw *that* he had come, but they also got a hint as to *why*. He came to be the perfect lamb, the ultimate, lasting sacrifice. This baby's coming was to accomplish and establish peace between the God of all creation and his image-bearers who habitually rejected him.

And so it would be all his days.

From the manger in Bethlehem to the cross on Calvary, Jesus moved among the people, came into their homes, touched their blind eyes, and permitted their unfaithful hands to touch him. He taught them profound lessons from ordinary events. He defended the defenseless and

---

[6] Mt 5:2–12

opposed the self-righteous. He ate at their tables, laughed with their children, and wept over their grief.

Never did he abandon his purpose for coming, which was to die for a world of spirit-poor outsiders as the Lamb of God who takes their sin away. Jesus was born poor. He lived poor. And he died poor for the sake of his people.

The shepherds could not have known that this boy came into this world in the same way he would leave it: out in the open, among the outcast, poor, and despised, but driven by one purpose—to ransom captive Israel that mourns in lonely exile until the Son of God appears.

When the shepherds arrived that night, looking to Mary and Joseph like men who had just encountered the angel of the Lord, they wanted to do more than see the baby. They wanted to behold the Lamb of God who takes away the sins of the world.

And that was the One whom they saw. But what they couldn't have known at the time was that though he was rich, for their sake he became poor, so that by his poverty they might become rich.[7]

---

[7] 2 COR 8:9

23

ONE STAR LIT FOR THEM

MATTHEW 2:1–12

N THE MONTHS after the census, Joseph and Mary stayed in Bethlehem, making their home there.[1] Meanwhile, learned men from the east, experts in the study of sacred texts, had heard that somewhere in Judea a boy had been born king of the Jews. They remembered that the Jewish holy book said, "A star shall come out of Jacob, and a scepter shall rise out of Israel."[2]

So when they saw a new star rise in the west, an uncommon one that seemed to have been lit just for them, they followed it. It led them to Jerusalem. Wanting to honor this king and pay tribute to his majesty, they began to ask around. Where was he?

Herod the Great was a paranoid sociopath—a personality perfect for his position as the ruler of Judea under the authority of Rome. He built his empire to create the illusion that he was a man who could be in many places at the same time. In addition to his fortresses at Herodium,

---

[1] MT 2:11   [2] NUM 24:17

Sebaste, Machaerus, and Masada, he also built palaces in Caesarea, Jericho, and Jerusalem. At any moment, he could have been in any one of them, so at every moment, he might as well have been in all of them. His affinity for architecture was well known, as was his obsessive mistrust of those around him.

There could only be one ruler in Judea. This was Herod's passionate commitment. Already the bones of one wife, several sons, and multiple distant relatives cluttered the family tomb as the result of his conviction that each and every one of them was involved in a conspiracy to kill him.

When he heard of these learned men and their quest, the dissonance of the words "king" and "Jews" with no mention of himself was more than he could stand. To Herod, the solution wasn't that complicated. If it meant killing every last baby boy in Israel, then that was what he would do. He called the chief priests and the scribes to tell him everything they knew about this king, smoldering with the feeling that they had been holding out on him.

Herod summoned them, seeking a theology lesson, and the priests gave him the details without confusion or hesitation: the prophet Micah said that the Messiah would be born in Bethlehem, just a few miles south, where Jacob's love Rachel was buried and where King David had been born. The chief priests were the keepers of the temple and of the religious life and culture of the Jews. The scribes, or teachers of the law, were the guardians of the Word of God. They wrote out copies of the sacred scriptures, poring over every last jot and tittle. They knew the minute details of every scroll of every book. They knew the lore. Still, curiously, not one of them seemed motivated to see for themselves if the Magi were right. They should have been the most expectant of the Messiah's coming, but all that the religious leaders displayed as they rehearsed these ancient prophetic details of their coming king was apathetic suspicion.

Jesus came to his own, and his own did not receive him.[3] They didn't seek him then, and they wouldn't seek him later either. Even when he was grown and ministering among them, they refused to believe in him.

But Herod believed. At least, enough to worry. He was one prone to err on the side of caution, and so it was enough for him that the Magi had come so far, laden with such gifts. And if there *was* such a king, maybe the Magi could lead him there. Maybe if he feigned a desire to bring a tribute of his own, the Magi would trust him and lead him to this new king.

"When you find him," Herod told the visitors, "come back and tell me where he is. I have a little something of my own I want to give him."[4]

After hearing him out, the Magi left for Bethlehem. It wasn't long before their familiar star rose again, leading them as a shepherd leads its sheep to a house on the outskirts of town.

When they found the king, it was no wonder he was nothing more than a murmur in Jerusalem. They entered the place where he lay and beheld a child in the arms of a young woman, practically still a girl. There was no crown or majesty that would attract them to him, no miracle they could see, no signs of greatness. Just a woman and her child. But there was something about that moment that only the woman, her husband, the Magi, and the child

---

[3] JN 1:11   [4] MT 2:8

knew—something that bent the knees of those scholars to the posture of worship when they saw him.

One of the Magi moved forward and produced a purse of gold, laying it at the child's feet. Another came with a flask of myrrh, then another with a box of frankincense. Unaware that they were funding a hasty trip to Egypt necessitated by Herod's paranoia, they gave these gifts for no other reason than to honor the one born King of the Jews.

He wasn't even *their* king. Israel's God was not their people's God. And yet, they had come because the thought of a God of mercy with healing in his wings awakened in them a desire to be close to the One through whom that healing would flow. They followed the star, and after countless miles of sojourn, they found the king.

It was quite a feat. They would rest well.

But that night as they drifted into a deep sleep of satisfaction, an angel, unfamiliar to them but well known to Mary, stepped into their dreams and painted for them the bloody truth of who Herod really was and what he meant to do to this baby. The angel warned them to take another route home.[5]

Herod's motives were murderous. History would remember him dripping not only with the blood of his own wives and sons, but with the blood of countless others, mostly boys under the age of two.

But not this boy king. Herod would not take his life.[6]

The Magi departed for home in secret, avoiding the area around Jerusalem.

For most of the residents of Bethlehem, Jesus' birth went unnoticed, but heaven and earth converged in this

---

[5] MT 2:12   [6] JN 10:18

little pocket of the Promised Land for the most important birth in history. The angels orchestrated the unlikely
meeting of the poor, the displaced, and the curious to
announce the coming of the Savior of the world. To some
they appeared in dreams. To others they spoke from the
sky. To others still, perhaps they shone like a star, leading
the Magi to the place where the child was born. Through it
all, the angels of the heavenly host had their eyes fixed on
this village south of Jerusalem.

Since the fall of man, God's promise to redeem and
restore has permeated the air and found its way into the
lyrics of kings and criminals. It has been the anthem of the
helpless, blind, lame, and guilt-ridden—a song of hope in
the night, rolling in from some distant country with the
trace of a melody known by heart.

In the pasture-lands outside Bethlehem, this song rose
like a celestial orchestra, crashing, singing, resounding
with the music, holding nothing back. Then all at once, as
with the fall of a curtain, the night fell silent, and the audience went back to their homes. Bethlehem went back to
being the ordinary town it had been for as long as anyone
could remember.

But the world would never be the same.

24

THE HEARTS OF MANY REVEALED

Luke 2:22–35

HE OLD MAN was a member of the old guard, the last of a generation of faithful ministers in Jerusalem's temple. He was something of a fixture—the kind of man who seemed to have always been there. It was hard to say whether Simeon smelled like the temple or the temple smelled like Simeon, but the minds of those who passed him in the street would often drift to notions of smoke and blood and a guilty resolve to attend to their worship more regularly.

The old guard to which he belonged was on a permanent watch. They were waiting for something in particular, something unique, something wonderful. The years had taught Simeon patience, so he was good at waiting. Still, he felt an unrelenting sense of urgency. He always had. He was waiting for the consolation of his people Israel. He had been waiting a long time, and his people even longer.

They were a nation of sorrows, acquainted with grief. They were despised, afflicted by God. They were wounded. They'd been crushed. They were like sheep that were better at getting lost than staying near their shepherd. And they needed consolation.

God would send it. And when he did, Simeon would be at his post, watching and waiting, poised to respond. This was his life's work. Simeon was a case study in the benefits of careful examination and devotion to the word of God. He was devout—a description best reserved for the aged. He knew how to *want* what God had promised. He knew how to delight in God's goodness. And he knew how to wait.

He worked in the temple because he believed God was near. He *knew* God was near. He knew this because God had visited him, telling him he wouldn't die before he had seen the Lord's Christ.[1] And at his age, it would have to be soon.

JOSEPH AND MARY were young, but they were believers. The generations before had taught them well. They journeyed to the temple for two reasons, both ancient—Mary's ritual purification after childbirth and the redemption of their firstborn son from the Lord.

Why did they need to redeem their son? Because God said in his law, "Consecrate to me all the firstborn. Whatever is the first to open the womb among the people of Israel, both of man and of beast, is mine."[2]

The consecration of the firstborn son was much more than a shallow routine asking God to give the child a long and happy life. They were recalling their history of slavery and deliverance from Egypt, where God traded the blood of a lamb for the blood of their firstborn sons—a life for a life.

This was the basis of God's claim that the firstborn sons belonged to him. When the parents accepted the sacrifice

---

[1] Lk 2:26   [2] Ex 13:1–2

of the lamb on their son's behalf, they forfeited their son's life to God, along with every generation that would flow from him. From that point on, when any first son was born to a descendant of those families, the parents brought that boy to the temple to present him to God because he belonged to God. The parents presented the boy in order to purchase his release and buy him back.[3]

Joseph and his wife answered the call of their ancient faith to observe the rite of purification for Mary and to redeem their son. Dark flecks of iron-scented blood spattered Mary's garments as the priest sprinkled her. Stained now with the fresh blood of her sacrifice, she was pronounced clean by the priest.

Then she and her husband took up their boy. It was time to purchase his release with more blood. As they moved toward the place where he would be redeemed, they passed an old man with searching eyes and purpose in his step.

He clearly belonged in the temple. He looked official. He smelled official. But as he drew near, they could hear him mumbling. He reached for the child. Mary, surprised but willing, handed over the boy.

Simeon's joyful hope was in the promise of a glimpse of the Christ, but God had something better in mind. Simeon actually got to *hold* him. This mumbling member of the old guard took this new life into his arms as his words rose to a cry of praise.

"O Lord, my God! Father of all blessing and honor and praise, you have been so good to your servant. You have been *so good* to your servant! I'm an old man, my days have been long, but I'm your son. And today, you have

---

[3] Ex 13:13–15

blessed me. I can't believe how good you've been! Do you see this boy? Do you see him? Because I see him, Father. And what's more, I know who he is. As surely as I live and breathe, I'm holding in my arms the Redeemer. With my very eyes I'm beholding your salvation, which you have prepared in the presence of a dark but watching world. He will be the light by which the Gentiles will see you and come to know you. He will be the light by which your people Israel will again see the glory of how you have loved them with a love that will not let them go. O great and glorious King, Shepherd of My Soul, Captain of My Guard, I have kept my post. I have not turned my eyes from the horizon because you have promised that your Messiah would come on my watch. And I have seen him. I have held him. I have kissed him. Now I can die in peace. So honorably retire your watchman, O great and glorious King, and bring me home."[4]

Joseph and Mary were speechless. They weren't expecting Simeon, and his blessing wasn't the standard fare. Most blessings were marked by warm petitions for success in life, but Simeon's wasn't a petition at all. It was a proclamation. He wasn't asking for what might be. He was declaring what was. Every word spoke to this child's purpose. There was something this child had come to do. They had brought Jesus to this place to redeem him, but before them stood a man proclaiming that this baby would, in fact, redeem them.

As his words sank in, Mary and Joseph marveled at what he had said. This moment was a meeting of hearts. For Simeon, the white-hot coal burning in him was finally exposed and began to die out. This was a happy moment.

---

[4] Lk 2:29–32

But his smile faded. The joy never left his eyes, but gravity pulled at his countenance. He grew serious. There was more to say because there was more to this little life than met the eye. All that Simeon had said so far was about what Jesus would *do*. Now it was time to broach the subject of *how* he would do it.

Simeon had a sense of what awaited Jesus. He told Mary a truth she must have already sensed: that Jesus would turn this world on its ear—and it would come at a great cost. Her baby would facilitate the ruin of many in Israel. Like a stump from Jesse's root, he would jut out and break the toes of any who dared tread upon the purpose for which he had come. Jesus would reveal the hearts of all mankind. The light of the world would shine in every dark corner of every dark heart, exposing every dark secret. And this was a world that had grown quite fond of darkness. It was no surprise that he would be opposed.[5]

He told her all these things, but she couldn't help suspecting that he was holding something back. There was something else on his mind. Something less general, more pointed—pointed at *her*.

And she was right. He had something to say, something that would hurt. But it had to be said, and he was the one appointed to say it. Simeon leveled his wrinkled face to look directly into the young mother's eyes.

"Mary, what awaits your son will be like a sword that will pierce through your soul."[6]

If Mary kept things spoken about Jesus in her heart, this must have been one of them. A sword would pierce her soul. It was the price of being the mother of the Christ. She had to raise this baby, knowing that he belonged to

---

[5] Lk 2:34   [6] Lk 2:35

the Maker and had come for the purpose of saving God's people from their sin. Everything in her culture told her that sin offerings were a bloody business. And thirty-three years later, she would find herself at the foot of the cross on which her son hung. With her own two eyes, she would watch him die, despised and rejected, a man of sorrows acquainted with grief.[7]

If her son was the salvation of Israel, then he was her savior too. Later, when he was a man, she must have thought about the way he talked of God's salvation. The way he spoke with such authority. "No one *takes* my life from me. But I lay it down of my own accord. And I alone have God's authority to lay it down and his authority to take it up again. This is why he sent me."[8]

There was purpose behind everything her son ever did. It was in his words. It was in his ways. It even seemed that he hung on that cross because he *meant* to. Her son wasn't simply dying. He was *doing* something.

---

[7] Isa 53:3, Jn 19:16–27   [8] Jn 10:18

25

THE THEME OF
MY SONG

MATTHEW 3:13–17

ESUS STEPPED INTO the river and made his way toward his cousin. "Baptize me, John."

John resisted. "Me baptize you? I should be baptized *by* you."

But Jesus said, "John, do as I ask. This moment marks the beginning of something greater than you can see."[1]

So John baptized the one whose trail he had come to blaze.[2]

When Jesus came out of the water, the Spirit of the Lord descended like a dove and came to rest on him as light flooded the valley. Then God spoke from the heavens: "This is my beloved Son, in whom I am well pleased."[3]

Though most who came to John for baptism were coming to repent, Jesus wasn't. He knew no sin.[4] He had come to stand in the place of people whose brokenness ran so deep that even their repentance was near-sighted and incomplete. Every facet of his life would be lived toward

---

[1] Mt 3:13–15   [3] Mt 3:17
[2] Lk 3:4   [4] 2 Cor 5:21

this end, to stand in the place of sinful people as their perfect substitute. This was his mission, the reason he had come. And it pleased the Lord.

John and Jesus stood in waters that had long been for their people a symbol of passing from one era to another. Generations earlier, the Lord had led his people out of their slavery in Egypt to the banks of this river. On that day the Lord had pushed back the Jordan's flow so that Joshua could usher his people into the land of their inheritance.[5]

On this day the Lord pushed back a torrent greater than a thousand rivers. This new Joshua would escort his people from the flood of their sorrows and pain to their eternal home. It would cost him dearly, but he would pay that price for the sake of love. More than a prophet, more than a priest, more than a king, Jesus was the beloved Son of God who had come to offer up his body to be broken for people who desperately needed it but didn't deserve it and couldn't earn it.

In those days it wasn't uncommon for men to claim that they were on an important mission from God. Some came promising military victories, others intellectual insight, others secret spiritual revelations unknown to the rest of the world. These self-appointed prophets inevitably picked up a few followers along the way—people willing to risk looking foolish on the off chance that this leader could give them the thing they wanted most.

But Jesus was different. There in the river at the beginning of his earthly ministry, it wasn't Jesus who claimed he'd been sent by God. God himself said it. The purpose of Jesus was the purpose of God. He didn't send his son to introduce a new religion but to fulfill the deepest needs and richest promises of an ancient one.

---

[5] JOSH 3:14–17

Since Adam and Eve ate the fruit God told them not to touch, every generation had groaned with the pains of childbirth, longing to be delivered from the effects of their first parents' fall.[6] And now their deliverer had come. He was the hero of their story, the perfect spotless lamb sent to adorn the doorposts of their hearts with his own blood.[7]

He was the descendant from Eve sent to crush the head of the deceiver.[8] He was Isaac's ram caught in the thicket, God's perfectly timed provision of a substitute.[9] He was the heir of Abraham's line through whom all the nations of the earth would be blessed—born by a miracle and filling the world with laughter.[10]

He wrestled with Israel and wouldn't let go, giving Jacob the gracious gift of a limp to remind him of his weakness.[11] He was the new Joseph, the forgotten brother, unrecognizable in a foreign land,[12] though he alone possessed the resources needed to satisfy the hunger of his people in their spiritual famine.

He was their new Moses, sent by God to deliver them from the land of their slavery into their promised inheritance.[13] He wouldn't just deliver God's Law to them.[14] He would fulfill it on their behalf. Perfectly.[15]

He was the faultless judge who would rescue his people from their own waywardness.[16] He would do what no other judge before him was able to do—he would take their hearts of stone and give them hearts of flesh.[17]

He was the king the Lord promised to David, a ruler from his own body whose Kingdom the Lord would

---

[6] Rom 8:22

[7] 1 Pet 1:17–21, Ex 12:22

[8] Gen 3:15

[9] Gen 22:13

[10] Gen 22:18

[11] Gen 32:25

[12] Gen 42:8, Jn 1:11

[13] Ex 3:7–10

[14] Ex 34:29

[15] Mt 5:17

[16] Jdg 2:17, 2 Cor 3:4–6

[17] Ezk 11:19

establish forever, ancient and strong.[18] He had courage deeper than David,[19] wisdom greater than Solomon,[20] and faith firmer than Elijah.[21] He was the remnant growing beneath the smoldering ruins of Judah, the son to be given, the child to be born.[22]

He was Immanuel—God with his people.[23] He would turn the hearts of fathers to their children and the hearts of children to their fathers.[24] Where there was despair, he would bring hope. Where there was brokenness, he would bring healing. Where there was sadness, he would bring joy. Where there was bondage, he would set people free.

But how much of this should the people at the Jordan that day have understood? How well could they have known the reasons Jesus pleased his Father? Great are the thoughts of God and vast the sum of them.[25] The people had grown up with the true tall tale of Immanuel's coming, they'd heard the prophets implore them to listen, but seeing, they did not see, and hearing, they did not hear, nor did they understand.[26]

But how could they? To whom have the plans of the Lord been revealed? Jesus would grow up like a young plant, like a root out of dry ground with nothing in his form—no majesty or beauty—that would lead anyone to desire him. He would be despised and rejected by men, a man of sorrows acquainted with grief. He would be like one from whom men hide their faces, despised and without esteem.[27]

No one could know by looking at him that he had come to bear their grief and carry their sorrows. The days

---

[18] 2 Sam 7:12
[19] Lk 6:1–5
[20] Lk 11:31
[21] Mt 4:1–11
[22] Isa 9:6
[23] Isa 6:13
[24] Mal 4:6
[25] Ps 139:17
[26] Mt 13:13
[27] Isa 53:1–3

ahead for him would bring suffering so great that people would consider him stricken by God and afflicted. But the purpose of this suffering was what pleased the Father. He would be wounded for their transgressions. He would be crushed for their iniquities. Upon him would be laid the punishment that would bring his people peace.[28] By his wounds they would be healed.[29]

Like sheep, every last man, woman, and child had gone astray, each turning to their own way. So the Father sent his Son and laid on him the iniquity of them all. When the time came, Jesus was oppressed and afflicted, but he didn't defend himself. Like a lamb led to the slaughter, he didn't open his mouth.[30] Under unjust allegations, Jesus was betrayed, arrested, tried, and put to death as a criminal. But death could not hold him. He had done no violence. He owed it no wage. So as he predicted, he was handed over to die, but three days later he rose from the grave.[31]

In all of this, Jesus was never the victim of men. No one took his life from him.[32] It was the will of his Father to crush him. It was God who put him through such grief to bear the iniquities of his people, making many unrighteous men righteous.[33]

As with his baptism, in his life and in his death Jesus stood in the place of the heartbroken and lost. Though this world had never known a greater teacher or more righteous example of how to live, Jesus' ministry was more than a ministry of words. He was born of a woman because he had come to do something his people couldn't do for themselves—bear their sins in his own body on the cross.[34]

---

[28] ROM 5:1, HEB 9:22   [31] HOS 6:2, 1 COR 15:3–4   [34] 1 PET 2:24
[29] ISA 53:4–5   [32] JN 10:18
[30] ISA 53:6–7   [33] ISA 53:8–12

Though no one could have known all of this at the time, Jesus was the priest who became the sacrifice, the king who took on the form of a servant, the prophet who himself was the Word of God.[35] He was Immanuel, God with us[36]—Son of God, Son of Man.[37]

But the death and resurrection of Jesus only makes sense through the lens of his birth. God's eternal Son, who was present at creation when God made man in his likeness,[38] humbled himself and took on flesh, born in the likeness of man.[39] The Maker knitted him together in Mary's womb, fearfully and wonderfully forming each tiny part in the depths of her waters. God saw his unformed body. Every day ordained for him was recorded in his Father's book of life before a single one had come to pass.[40]

And now he has come.

Behold the Lamb of God who takes away the sins of the world.

—๛—

---

[35] Jn 1:1
[36] Isa 7:14, Mt 1:23
[37] Jn 20:31, Mt 12:40
[38] Gen 1:26
[39] Phil 2:7
[40] Ps 139:13–16

So rejoice, ye children, sing
And remember now his mercy
And sing out with joy
For the brave little boy is our Savior
Son of God,
Son of Man

Acknowledgments

I'VE ALWAYS WANTED to write. Without the help of many friends and colleagues, there's no way I could do it.

First, to Lisa: Your sacrifice has given me the gift of time, your love has given me the gift of confidence, and your friendship has given me the gift of joy. Thank you. I love you.

To Chris, Maggie, Kate, and Jane: You are among the greatest treasures I have ever known. You give so much more than you take. Please stop growing up.

To A. S. Peterson, Jennifer Trafton Peterson, Jessica Barnes, and Roy Roper: Thanks for all the heavy lifting you've done to take this book to print. Your input, encouragement, and eye for detail has taught me so much.

To the Rabbit Room community: Jamie Peterson and kids (Aedan, Asher, and Autumn), Randall and Amy Goodgame, Jonathan and Lou Alice Rogers (who know the difference between an anecdote and a remark), Matt Connor, Ron Block, Eric and Danielle Peters, Jason Gray, Evie Coates, S. D. Smith, Travis Prinzi, Father Thomas

McKenzie, Sarah Clarkson, Lanier Ivester, Andy Gulla-
horn, Jill Phillips, Ben and Beth Shive, Josh and Kirsten
Shive, Andy and Alison Osenga, and Justin Gerard. You
all inspire me to no end.

To Midtown Fellowship: Randy Draughon, Joel
Walker, Dave Burden, Chad and Carly Fair, Adrienne
Williams, John Haney, Kevin Mann, Hal Garrett, Jennifer
Butcher, Elizabeth Olmstead, Evy Brooks, and the con-
gregation at 12 South. You all are a gift. I marvel at God's
goodness when I think of you.

To Sally Lloyd-Jones, Charlie Peacock, Andi Ash-
worth, Scott Sauls, Donald Guthrie, Dan Doriani, Dan
Zink, Chuck Gifford, Scotty Smith, and Annie Dillard.
I've treasured your mentorship over the years.

To Rick and Laura Pierce: Thanks for the Ryman
tickets. I really hope you don't regret that move. Lisa and I
love you guys.

To our friends Travis and Rachel Keller: You guys have
brought out the best in Team Ramsey.

To Oak Hills Presbyterian Church: I love you and am
so thankful for you.

To Rich and Deb Wold: Thanks for Lisa. She's pretty
great.

To Dad, Mom, Ryan, Nancy, A.J., and Nathan: I
wouldn't trade my family for anyone. I have seen the hope
of Jesus shape each of your lives in ways that silence my
doubts. I love you.

And last but not least, to Andrew Peterson: Thank
you for caring to tell this story so well and for calling your
friends to come tell it with you. It is an honor to tell this
story, and it is an honor to call you friend.

John 21:17.

Special thanks to the Yodis family
for helping us bring this book into the world.

RABBIT ROOM
— P R E S S —

BOOKS. MUSIC. COMMUNITY.
WWW.RABBITROOM.COM

The stories are true.

CPSIA information can be obtained
at www.ICGtesting.com
Printed in the USA
LVHW02s0036241017
553515LV00002B/2/P